Work: A Very Short Introduction

VERY SHORT INTRODUCTIONS are for anyone wanting a stimulating and accessible way in to a new subject. They are written by experts, and have been published in more than 25 languages worldwide.

The series began in 1995, and now represents a wide variety of topics in history, philosophy, religion, science, and the humanities. The VSI library now contains more than 300 volumes—a Very Short Introduction to everything from ancient Egypt and Indian philosophy to conceptual art and cosmology—and will continue to grow in a variety of disciplines.

VERY SHORT INTRODUCTIONS AVAILABLE NOW:

Available soon:

For more information visit our website
www.oup.com/vsi/

Stephen Fineman

WORK

A Very Short Introduction

OXFORD
UNIVERSITY PRESS

Great Clarendon Street, Oxford, OX2 6DP,
United Kingdom

Oxford University Press is a department of the University of Oxford.
It furthers the University's objective of excellence in research, scholarship,
and education by publishing worldwide. Oxford is a registered trade mark of
Oxford University Press in the UK and in certain other countries

© Stephen Fineman 2012

The moral rights of the author have been asserted

First Edition published in 2012

Impression: 1

British Library Cataloguing in Publication Data

Data available

Library of Congress Cataloging in Publication Data

Data available

ISBN 978-0-19-969936-0

Printed in Great Britain by
Ashford Colour Press Ltd, Gosport, Hampshire

Acknowledgements

My special thanks to Caroline, Dave, Carol, Dan, and Anna.

Contents

Preface

The story of work is fascinating because it is the story of us—how we strive for security and reward and, for some of us, meaning and individuality. Work—paid or unpaid, voluntary or obligatory—is woven into the fabric of all human societies to become part of our identities and key to life's narrative. From an early age, it captures the imagination of children, prompted by '…and what do you want to be when you grow up?' type questions.

Different eras bring different work opportunities and choices: some types of work remain while others are superseded by economic upheavals or technological invention. Living is problematic, at the very least, without paid work; for many people it is catastrophic. Yet jobs are rarely fairly distributed and the personal rewards are hugely variable: we can love or hate our work, or simply endure it. Work can be literally a killer or, contrastingly, a source of much vitality and pleasure.

Many of us are experts about work because, in one form or another, we have done it—or seen others do it. These experiences inform our basic understandings, and are privileged in this book. But work does not exist in a social vacuum. It is influenced by our families, schools, economic ideologies, and workplace cultures—to mention but a few. In this book, I try to convey something of this mosaic by looking at work from both the inside and the outside. I speak as a social scientist, but a somewhat eclectic one. The sources I draw upon include psychology, sociology, anthropology, management, and social history, as well as popular media accounts.

List of illustrations

Chapter 1
Why work?

In many different ways, we all work. By this I mean that work, in its most general sense, is something that exercises our brain and brawn as we do things: the effort of cooking a meal, sweeping the floor, driving along a congested motorway, studying for an exam, cutting the grass, or downloading computer files. Whether or not we call it work is another matter. For some people a holiday can be hard work; their childcare both work and pleasure; their job feels like a hobby.

So the idea of what counts as work is, at one level, personal and idiosyncratic. We weave our own meanings and purposes from the threads of our daily endeavours. But none of this occurs in a cultural vacuum. Our cultures impress meanings onto us, shape our expectations and perceptions. What constitutes work, and its 'opposite', leisure, is culturally loaded. Culture establishes the kinds of work that should be remunerated and what should be freely given. It sets an order of prestige or status for different types of work. It determines the work that is more appropriate for a man or a woman, a child or an adult, the young or the old. But of course, cultural predilections do not always have their way—they can be resisted and eventually transformed, as history teaches us.

Working a regulated 9 to 5 day and separating it from non-work is a relatively recent phenomenon, a reaction to the very long working hours—up to sixteen hours a day for six days—that dominated the factory system of the Industrial Revolution. Measured hours were of little concern to industrial workers' early ancestors, the traditional hunter-gatherers. Apart from not having clocks, other rhythms shaped their working patterns. They characteristically continued their labours until there was enough food, and then they stopped. For example, before the Kalahari Bushmen of Southern Africa became conventional farmers of livestock and corn, they enjoyed an itinerant lifestyle of hunting and foraging, which could sometimes amount to no more than one day in every ten. Trading within the community was frowned upon, but the sharing of food, gift giving, and the regular swapping of stories about family, children, and hunting, cemented a rich social structure. Such activity could be regarded as a period for recovery from work and for leisure, but it was not seen that way by the Bushmen. The very division, work/leisure, was simply not relevant to how they constructed their lives and their sense of belonging.

Living time

A poignant example, which exposes the contrasts between modern and traditional working cultures, concerns the fate of a group of Brazilian Tapajos Indians. In the 1930s they were enrolled by Henry Ford in a venture of extraordinary hubris. He devoted his considerable fortune to the creation of his dream city, 'Fordlandia', in the midst of the Amazon rainforest. His eponymous city was designed to his precise specifications to look like a perfect American suburb (complete with church and movies), to attract and house local Tapajos workers along with their American managers. Their task was to cultivate a rubber plantation to serve the growing world market for latex, under the same authoritarian, highly regimented, management methods that had produced Ford's ubiquitous Model T motor car.

The project suffered a catalogue of setbacks, not least the response of the Tapajos workforce. Their traditional work pace had been set by the shifting seasons and the intensity of the sun, and they could normally produce all that they needed in the relatively dry months of June to November. As Greg Grandin, author of *Fordlandia*, observes: 'Before the coming of Ford, Tapajos workers lived time, they didn't measure it—most rarely ever heard church bells, much less a factory whistle. It was difficult [said a Ford labor recruiter] "to make 365-day machines out of these people". The simmering discontent of the workers exploded in an orgy of destruction, dramatically symbolized by the wrecking of the time clock that recorded their time of entry and exit each day.

The impulse to work—or not

Whether or not we call it 'work', in a formal sense, it is clear that any human community has to devise an economic system to feed and shelter itself—and that usually entails work. Beyond that, why we work, and precisely who does what, speaks much of the cultural norms and the structure of a society. In complex economies, divisions of work follow lines of gender, power, and privilege. Apart from their public duties, ancient Greeks regarded work as something to relegate to slaves, who were themselves divided by status—from chattel slave to free citizen. Ancient Rome, too, put slavery at the core of its economy. Farm estates of the era were typically staffed by slaves who were managed by a slave bailiff. Freedmen, former slaves who had been legally released from slavery, were hired by the wealthy to undertake craft trades, a task that freeborn Romans deemed beneath their dignity. The Roman elite (by dint of ancestry or property) would combine a life of ease with civic affairs, some within the higher ranks of the military. It was a time when territorial expansion secured riches and protection, as well as more slaves. Rome's generals had a flair for winning, and its administrators a talent for governance and exploitation. Today, pecking orders of who does what kind of work remain in all parts of globe, heavily influenced by social class, education, wealth, gender, race, age, or ethnicity.

Unravelling the reasons why we work has long challenged philosophers and social scientists. The clichéd answer, 'for money', is nicely tested when people suddenly win a great deal of money, more than enough to meet their usual needs. Some decide to continue in their old job, regardless. A news report of one lucky bus driver illustrates:

> Chorley dad who netted more than £2m on the lottery will not give up his day job as a bus driver—but he might go part time. Kevin Halstead, 46, has been driving the 125 bus between Bolton and Preston for the past 17 years and says he doesn't want to let winning £2,302,668 in last week's Lottery draw get in the way of his career.

This bus driver's behaviour is compatible with findings from surveys that pose questions of the sort: 'If you were to get enough money to live as comfortably as you would like for the rest of your life, would you continue to work or would you stop working?' Back in the 1950s, some 80 per cent of US respondents said that they would keep working; today the figure is rather lower at 70 per cent. In other words (and acknowledging that people do not always do what they say), the work ethic still appears reasonably robust in the USA. But there are some in the USA who read the numbers differently—as a worrying sign of decline in the spirit that has motivated the American Dream.

Work ethics

In 1905, the influential German sociologist Max Weber wrote a book titled *The Protestant Work Ethic and the Spirit of Capitalism*. In it, he argued that the Industrial Revolution and development of capitalism were formed around the strictures of seventeenth-century Protestantism. Hard work, duty, and obedience were religious obligations and essential to spiritual salvation; there was little time or tolerance for fun or leisure. It was a happy union of spirituality and self-interest for the industrial elite (but decidedly less so for rank-and-file workers, for whom it could be unremittingly brutish).

There is much to be said for Weber's analysis, drawing our attention to the religious roots that inspired early entrepreneurs. But Protestant preaching reveals only part of the religion-and-industry story. Other major religions embrace hard work, such as Islam, Buddhism, and Catholicism. The industrial development of Japan, Taiwan, China, and large parts of Europe can be seen to be, at least in part, a reflection of their different religions and the values that they enshrine. In practice, Jews became fine carriers of the sentiments that define the Protestant work ethic, well pre-dating Protestantism—despite the injunction in the Torah that work is basically a distraction from learning.

In today's multicultural societies, any general notion of a single work ethic is likely to be misguided. While work is firmly part of the social and political agenda of all industrial societies, the priority placed on getting a job, working hard, and striving to achieve is filtered by family, community, and ethnic values and pressures—which may or may not have a religious component. Moreover, as the work ethic has become increasingly secularized, other 'ethics' have entered the social arena.

There are pronouncements on people who appear wedded to a 'welfare ethic', seemingly keen to live off the social provision of the state. In recent years, long working hours have contributed to an 'overwork ethic', the vision of people tied to their desks, machines, or computers for all hours. In contrast, there is the 'leisure ethic', where relaxation and recreation are prioritized over long and concentrated work. Those who claim to live by it often describe their jobs in low-key terms: 'it's just a job' or 'a day's work for a day's pay'. Some leisure aficionados aim to work smarter, not harder, seeking ways of beating the system. As one enthusiast put it,

Old-fashion work ethics mean you should work hard to accomplish your goals, and doing it any other way is unethical. Blindly putting yourself to the grind is wrong in so many ways...If you can get the job done at a fraction of the time, then the rest of the time can be used to get more things accomplished, to spend it with family, or whatever else you see fit.

The generation link

Generational differences in work ethics have attracted much popular attention, and some research interest. The core proposition is that people who grow up in a particular period or era will share common experiences, which will distinctively mould their character and values for their lifetime. A workforce comprising mixed generations can, according to some writers, be problematic. At worst it leads to serious misunderstandings, resulting in conflict and inefficiency. A US business consultant, Cam Marston, asserts alarmingly that 'generation conflict costs billions of dollars in lost productivity to organizations like yours worldwide—not to mention the incalculable effects on motivation and moral'.

The generations are typically divided into four, each with a different work ethic. There is the Silent Generation, Baby Boomers, Generation X, and Generation Y. The Silent Generation was born in the 1920s and 1930s in times of economic recession, and is seen as conservative, conformist, and prepared to work fairly hard. Baby Boomers were born in the 1940s and 1950s, part of the regeneration and increasing affluence that occurred in some countries after the Second World War. They are results driven, loyal, and prepared to give maximum effort. Their offspring are Generation X, born between 1960 and the mid-1970s. They are portrayed as valuing informality and a work–life balance and, in the eyes of Baby Boomers, somewhat feckless and uncommitted to their work. Generation Ys—the 'Millennium Generation' (mid-1970s–mid-1990s) are 'bathed in bits', 'digital natives' who prefer collaborative working, have a strong urge for personal development and flexibility, and are keen to learn new skills. Their 'strangeness' and 'narcissism' can bewilder earlier generations, a view advanced in *Fortune* business magazine:

> Nearly every businessperson over 30 has done it: sat in his office after a staff meeting and—reflecting upon the 25-year-old colleague with two tattoos, a piercing, no watch and a shameless propensity for chatting up the boss—wondered, What is with that guy?!

Generalizing about a generation is attractive—an easy, but somewhat lazy, way of dividing populations into large chunks and assuming that all who fall into a particular category are similar—which often they are not. It also produces a self-fulfilling prophecy: we expect the generations to be different, therefore they *are* different. As most of us can point to some differences in outlook between children, parents, and grandparents, the notion that this must be generational is readily taken as obvious.

The extent to which these generational characterizations are worth their salt is, nevertheless, an open question. The few existing empirical studies that specifically test out their claims do locate some small differences. One is the higher premium placed on leisure time amongst Generation X and Generation Y workers. Compared to their predecessors, the centrality of work in their lives has declined and they—especially Generation X—are more preoccupied with status and money. More generally, though, the contention that generational differences in the workforce will produce an explosive mix should be regarded with caution. It is a handy rhetoric for some business consultants, but evidence suggests considerable overlap and mix between the generations, often resulting in mutual learning and understanding. Moreover, differences between generational cohorts are often eclipsed by the differences within a generational group.

Motivation matters

What spurs people on, or not, at work can be seen as a motivational question. Motivational explanations (from the Latin *emovere* 'to move') locate the spark of our energies within us, as part of our personalities. Wider social or generational influences are viewed as less crucial than one's individual psychology and personal make-up. An appeal of motivation, as a concept, is that it offers a ready sense of closure when we want to give *a* reason for behaviour, such as being motivated by greed, anxiety, lust, achievement, anger, jealousy, fear, or insecurity. The legitimacy of a court of law is derived, in part, from identifying 'a motive' for a crime.

But would it were so simple. Much human conduct, inside and outside of work settings, can be viewed as a mix of complex and often conflicting motives, some of which, if we acknowledge Sigmund Freud's considerable contribution, are unconscious. The nature of the 'actual' motive can be elusive and depend on who is interpreting the behaviour or making the judgement. The context is crucial. Your view that your colleague is being deliberately vindictive towards you can be countered by her denial; she says she was 'simply upset by the row she had with her boyfriend last night'. The 'true' motive—if there is one—slips between different accounts, rationalization, and attributions. It is a very social process.

We learn vocabularies of motive from an early age. They are social products; ways of explaining or labelling another's conduct or saying why we want or need something. The plausibility of the terminology we use depends on the circumstances. A young child soon learns that saying 'I'm really hungry' is more likely to produce food than 'I'm really greedy' (regardless of his or her biological need for sustenance). In work settings, motives can rapidly become politicized. A manager who sharply criticizes an employee's work 'just wants to help them perform better'. The employee, though, sees the manager as 'unkind and insulting'. As

I write, a long-standing dispute between British Airways and its cabin crew has finally been resolved. The cabin crew's trade union accused British Airways of being motivated by malice, using disciplinary procedures in a 'witch hunt'. British Airways managers, in turn, claimed the opposite; they had been 'very fair' in their approach and the union has 'nobody to blame but itself'. Putative motives were being traded in sharp, point-scoring, manoeuvres.

Many theories

Academic theories of motivation vary in their level of sophistication and complexity. They come in different guises (goal theory, expectancy theory, equity theory, two-factor theory, reactance theory, and attribution theory, to mention but a few). Some are now embedded in business and management education, often in skeletal form and rules of thumb on 'how to motivate people at work'.

A popular formulation is Douglas McGregor's Theory X and Theory Y. Writing in the 1960s, McGregor, an American professor of management, proposed that the key to understanding worker motivation lies in what managers assume of their staff. McGregor discerned two patterns. There were Theory X managers who believed that coercion, tight controls, and punishments worked best—given that workers disliked responsibility and were resistant to change. In contrast, Theory Y managers believed workers to be inherently self-directing and willing to take responsibility, so they responded best to liberal, empowering, forms of management. McGregor's intention was not to advocate the superiority of one form over the other, but to invite managers to reflect on their particular theory, X or Y, and its consequences. This was, perhaps, a touch naive as Theory Y was rapidly promulgated as the ideal perspective, reflecting the 1960s trend in humanizing management–worker relations. McGregor's approach remains catchy for its simplicity, and it is in tune with the current espousal (though not necessarily enactment) of Theory Y values. But, in essence, it tells us more about the stereotypes that are held by managers than about the different motivations of workers.

A more nuanced approach was taken by Abraham Maslow. Maslow's 'general theory of motivation' appeared in the 1940s, built upon the foundations of existing 'need theory' and refined from his research as a humanistic psychologist in the USA. A need perspective is relatively straightforward. We are characterized as having different, individual, needs, some biological, others learned and social. If unmet, the need will trigger a drive or motive—a mechanism to keep the human organism in balance. Should the process fail, we may seek a substitute goal, or be left with feelings of tension or frustration to internalize, or express as irritation, anger, or rage. From this standpoint, there is always a reason and purpose behind what we do or, as sociologist Tony Watson puts it: 'The person is seen as a little machine-like system in which goals or "motives" operate as a motor "powering" the human entity so that it behaves in a particular way.'

Maslow's core contribution was to argue that our needs are not randomly distributed, but are arranged in hierarchical sets (Figure 1). As one set of needs becomes relatively satisfied, we are motivated, driven, to move to the next set, and progressively towards the apex of the pyramid, which Maslow termed self-actualization—'to be all that we are able to be'. Food, air, water, and sleep meet our most basic, physiological needs, followed by safety, stability, and security. As the prospect of loneliness looms, it is allayed by social contacts and loving friends and partners. Respect from others and social status then become preoccupations. During life changes or crises, such as illness, injury, or unemployment, we can move down or up the hierarchy, but its pinnacle is self-actualization, a dynamic state of continuous self-improvement.

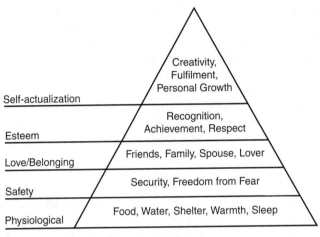

Food, Water, Shelter, Warmth, Sleep — Physiological

Security, Freedom from Fear — Safety

Friends, Family, Spouse, Lover — Love/Belonging

Recognition, Achievement, Respect — Esteem

Creativity, Fulfilment, Personal Growth — Self-actualization

1. Abraham Maslow's 'hierarchy of needs'

Maslow wanted his theory to apply universally, but it is very much a product of the achieving/professional American culture of which Maslow himself was a part. Many jobs simply do not have the potential for self-actualization, while lack of empirical support for the theory has bothered many psychologists. It should, for example, be applied with caution to ethnic and teenage groups with value systems that can depart markedly from Maslow's particular conception. There are, moreover, individual lifestyles that are compelling exceptions to the hierarchal rule, such as creative artists who live on the economic edge yet produce extraordinary work, and religious missionaries who work alone and precariously. The cultural slant is evident when cross-cultural comparisons are made, such as Scandinavians' emphasis on social needs more than self-actualization, and Chinese prioritization of safety and security.

Maslow's ideas—like McGregor's—have been a seductive response to the dehumanizing and alienating climate that has surrounded much industrial work. They have offered managers a simple, if simplistic, basis for rethinking their styles of management and the incentives that they can provide. Even though scientifically shaky, Maslow's theory continues to be canvassed within managerial circles and retains rhetorical force. Today's human resource managers have at their disposal different ways of arranging workplace conditions and rewards that, in principle, could be attuned to Maslow's hierarchy, at least in part: pay, pensions, and job security to meet the lower-level needs; team membership and workgroup composition at the middle level; and, for a some jobs, enhancing the scope for achievement and self-actualization.

Reorientations

The difficulties in applying motivational theories have led some workplace researchers away from speculating on the deeper roots of motivation, and more towards people's attitudes, or *orientations*, to their work: the expectations that they bring with them to the workplace.

The notion of orientation to work was initially advanced by John Goldthorpe and his colleagues in the 1960s to account for the shifting attitudes of affluent members of the working class in the UK. The researchers found that some workers were distinctly *instrumental* and calculative; they had no interest in self-actualizing at work or for making friends there: work was a means to different ends and attractions, beyond the workplace. Others were more *bureaucratic* in orientation, keen to serve the organization and to blur the line between work and non-work. The last group were *solidaristic*; having a strong moral sense of where the interests of the firm should lie, especially in representing worker rights and unionization. They held a 'them and us' passion that they carried readily into their non-work life. Variations on these orientations have been found in recent studies, attesting to the survival and development of an important concept—and also a lingering chicken-and-egg question. Are orientations to work formed *before* entering work, or are they shaped from *being* at work? Or perhaps both?

Chapter 2
A spectrum of jobs

Work can be divided broadly into what is officially counted and what is not. The latter fails to appear in Gross National Product statistics, yet is fundamental to the economic and cultural complexion of society. It contains what is loosely termed 'the domestic sphere'—the everyday 'free' labour of bringing up your child, doing housework, fixing your own plumbing, or caring for a sick or elderly relative. It also includes the considerable 'white' economy of unpaid volunteers who, amongst other things, provide care to vulnerable people, run youth groups, and work for charitable organizations. The black economy completes the picture—a murky zone of private cash transactions, criminal activity, and unregulated, unprotected, workers.

When jobs are unattainable, scarce, or illegal, the black economy proliferates. It is estimated that some 10 per cent of the USA's economy is made up in this way, people who work as maids, nannies, or taxi drivers, or in back-street sweatshops. In developing countries that face endemic unemployment, the black economy can be the only place to find work and a meagre income—such as the street vendor, rickshaw driver, or child scrap-hunter (Figure 2). The criminal black economy operates surreptitiously and often ruthlessly—such as in child trafficking, drug dealing, sex work, and illegal migrant labour. Its victims typically go unnoticed and unrecorded. Guo Bin Long was an

2. A child scavenging rubbish from trucks before they unload at a
Philippines landfill site

exception. He was an illegal Chinese immigrant to the UK, trafficked to Morecambe Bay by a wealthy Chinese gang master to harvest valuable sea cockles. Guo Bin Long was indentured to this man for his squalid, overcrowded, accommodation as well as to Snakehead gangs in China for his passage costs. In 2004, along with twenty others, he perished as the notorious Morecambe Bay tide engulfed him. He made a last desperate call on his mobile phone to his wife, some 5,000 miles away: 'I am up to my chest in water. Maybe I am going to die... Tell the family to pray for me. It's too close. I am dying.'

The criminal black economy takes no prisoners, exploiting the vulnerable and unwary with little-to-no protection. As it grows, it can consume from within the very foundations of a nation's economy—exemplified by the long battle with the Mafia in Italy and the USA, and the continuing drug wars in Mexico.

Jobs in the formal economy

The formal economy provides jobs that are legally constituted within a country's tax and employment laws (on hours of work, minimum wage, safety, health insurance, pensions, holiday entitlement, and maternity/paternity leave). 'Formal economy' is a bland term for a remarkable and changing array of jobs that tell us much about a culture and its times. Jobs in Victorian Britain, for example, offer a tantalizing glimpse of the livelihoods, language, and priorities of the era, such as:

Ale draper: seller of ale
Alnager: official who examined the quality of woollen goods
Ankle beater: young person who helped to drive the cattle to market
Bagniokeeper: in charge of a bath house or brothel
Beaver: made felt used in hat making
Campaner: bell maker
Carner: granary keeper

Xylographer: user and maker of wooden blocks used in printing illustrations

Quister: someone who bleached things

Lorner: maker of horse gear

Nob thatcher: maker of wigs

Orrery maker: made a mechanical device for showing the movements of the planets

Upright worker: chimney sweep

Ratoner: rat catcher

Hacker: maker of hoes, axes, and other cutting tools

Many of these jobs have now disappeared or transformed; a few have changed radically in meaning (a hacker now serving—or soiling—the computing world). Today's jobs encompass no less than 4,000 different titles, according to the International Labour Office. They encapsulate the eccentricities, fashions, and technological preoccupations of our age, such as ATM servicer, data input clerk, daycare provider, financial manager, GPS car-navigator installer, laser cutter operator, and missile officer. Each national census removes jobs that have become defunct, and adds new ones, such as the following ten in the UK's 2011 census:

Colon hydrotherapist: an individual who practises colonic irrigation

Environmental psychologist: an individual who investigates the relationship between people and their physical environment

Forensic accountant: an accountant involved in work relating to engagements resulting from actual or anticipated disputes or litigation

Abseiler: a person who descends down a nearly vertical face by using a doubled rope that is wrapped around the body and attached to some high point

Leakage technician: is responsible for trying to locate leaks in the water network

Feng shui consultant: a person who positions objects, especially graves, buildings, and furniture, based on a belief in patterns of yin and yang and the flow of chi that have positive and negative effects

Pole dancer: someone who will dance on a pole for money

Reiki healer: energy therapy healer. Can be achieved through looking, blowing, light tapping and touching, to give energy

Acoustician: an expert in acoustics

eBay trader: someone who runs a business through selling and buying on eBay

Knowledge work

As advanced economies have become more specialized and competitive, there has been a move away from investments in machines, buildings, and equipment—hard, physical, assets— towards knowledge-intensive work. Management writer Peter Drucker signalled the change in the late 1960s: 'Today the center is the knowledge worker, the man or woman who applies to productive work ideas, concepts, and information rather than manual skill or brawn.' Of course, every job requires knowledge, so it could be said that everyone is, and always has been, a knowledge worker. But the knowledge economy places particular emphasis on the economic value of people who are intellectually skilled, good at abstract thinking and solving non-standardized problems—the hallmarks of creativity and innovation. They include professional knowledge workers such as lawyers, doctors, diplomats, law makers, and software developers. High-end knowledge workers in large corporations have become especially valued, such as strategy formulators, product designers, and marketing executives. The growth of the knowledge economy has raised the profile of advanced educational programmes, specialist training, and 'lifelong learning'.

Estimates of the proportion of knowledge workers in the labour force vary between 28 per cent and 45 per cent. A study by *The Work Foundation* in 2006 concluded that the UK had a 30–30–40 workforce. Thirty per cent of jobs were knowledge intensive and represented the core of knowledge workers—professional leaders, innovators, and experts. Another 30 per cent had some knowledge content and included care workers, information handlers, servers, and sellers. The remaining 40 per cent contained little knowledge work; they were mainly operators, assistants, and clerks.

Status and worth

A job has long been a key locator of a person's socioeconomic standing or social class—subjective and objective. Although some cultures are less bound by social class divisions than others, population demographers typically depict the social classes in up to six different bands. In the *upper class* are typically owners of considerable land or stock, top executives, celebrities, royalty, and powerful politicians. The *upper middle class* includes professionals and managers. The *lower middle class* incorporates the semi-professional and craftspeople. The *working class* are blue collar and clerical workers (people, in Marxian terms, who have to sell their physical labour for wages and have no ownership of the means of production). The *lower class* are those in poorly paid work who have limited participation in the labour force. Finally, there is the *underclass*, victims of poverty who are excluded from participation in legitimate economic activities.

We may or may not identify with the social class to which we are officially assigned. Subjective, or 'felt', class is as much about personal identity, which can include, but also transcend, occupation. It typically reflects one's family background, educational attainment, peer pressure, and social image—the cachet or stigma of describing oneself as belonging to a particular social class. In the *Annual Survey of British Social Attitudes* in 2007, nearly 60 per cent of a large random sample regarded themselves as working class, even though half of them did not work in blue collar jobs. The disconnect is revealed in individual stories:

> I was born working class (21-year-old dad as head of household was a labourer). Dropped to 'underclass' (single parent on benefits). She [my mother] remarried a photographer (lower middle class) and now I'm a teacher (middle class). My social habits (football + pubs)

and voting patterns are working class. But I enjoy international travel + museum visits (M/C). Is it any wonder I'm developing a multiple personality disorder.

I had a very middle class upbringing and was labelled posh at school. I didn't go to university and now manage a project and rent my house. My working class friends invariably have university degrees and own their own homes—they describe themselves as working class and I finally have the guts to say I'm middle class (according to my background and belief systems). But which of us is correct?

I suppose I'm middle class—being a teacher with a university degree and having had parents who both were graduates too. But I go out to work every day...so I'm working class really. And I have good manners and speak clearly enough for other people to understand me and have a coat of arms, so maybe I'm upper class. The whole thing is silly and outmoded.

Money

Generally, higher socioeconomic class workers are rewarded with higher pay—but not always. Social position mixes with market forces and cultural fashions to determine a worker's financial value. Figure 3 shows the income hierarchy for a number of occupations in the UK.

It is noteworthy that, on average, the salary of a top football manager greatly exceeds that of a prime minister. A stockbroker earns some forty-five times as much as a nurse, social worker, or firefighter, while a senior management consultant can earn twice as much as a doctor, and four times the salary of a higher education teacher. All are indicators of how cultural and market ideologies can shape, and some would say distort, our social priorities. They raise fundamental questions about the moral muteness of the 'the market' in distributing financial rewards, and its ability to ride roughshod over the intrinsic goodness, effort, or personal risk associated with a job. The 'bonus culture' in some

Premier league football manager	£3,230,000
Partner of major management consultancy firm	£167,950
Directors and chief executives of major organizations	£151,046
Prime minister	£142,500
Stockbrokers	£115,612
Financial managers	£83,396
Medical practitioners	£76,000
Aircraft pilots and flight engineers	£68,582
Solicitors and lawyers, judges and coroners	£54,277
IT strategy and planning professionals	£48,512
Train drivers	£41,176
Higher education teaching professionals	£39,372
Police officers (sergeant and below)	£38,804
Primary and nursery education teaching professionals	£30,548
Social workers	£28,594
Fire service officers (leading fire officer and below)	£26,863
Nurses	£25,800
Countryside and park rangers	£20,677
Refuse and salvage occupations	£18,339
Call centre agents/operators	£15,160
Care assistants and home carers	£13,289
Fitness instructors	£11,236
Hairdressers, barbers	£10,832
Retail cashiers and check-out operators	£9,872
Floral arrangers, florists	£9,597
Cleaners, domestics	£8,133
Waiters, waitresses	£7,602

3. What are they worth? UK average annual salaries, 2010

industries, especially financial services, has added fuel to the debate: top executives granted million-dollar bonuses on top of million-dollar salaries. In recent years, payments have been grossly out of step with the rest of the economy and, for some executives, tantamount to a 'reward for failure': they have presided over declining businesses.

Power plays

Since the eighteenth century, workers have sought to protect their interests by forming trade unions, following in the footsteps of the merchant and craft guilds of medieval Europe. Today, Sweden tops the union membership tables with nearly 80 per cent of its workforce unionized, compared to the UK's 30 per cent, the USA's 12 per cent, and France's 8 per cent. The large differences reflect contrasting ideologies about workplace relations, different regimes of legal enforcement, as well as the union movement's diminishing coherence in some countries. In the West, employees are normally free to join a union should they desire, and there are many employers that recognize a union's right to negotiate working conditions. But there are notable exceptions: Toyota, Honda, the John Lewis Partnership, FedEx, and Marks & Spencer, for instance, have held unions at distance, relying on their own brands of industrial democracy to achieve equitable agreements.

Industrial democracy is an umbrella term to describe the means and extent of employee participation in organizational decision-making—on issues such as company performance, job security, and working conditions. In Europe it is common to find works councils taking on these issues, some run by management, some by workers, some by unions. In practice, industrial democracy ranges from the cosmetic to the substantive, the latter more likely when ownership is broadly distributed amongst employees, such as in cooperatives. The 70,000 employees of the UK's John Lewis Partnership, for example, are co-owners of the business, and there is a cascade of internal consultative mechanisms to ensure a wide spread of decision-making. The firm has attracted much praise in the business press, some eulogizing it as a workers' paradise. But industrial democracy remains a slippery concept, with different meanings to different people. Even the John Lewis Partnership fails to satisfy some academic critics, who claim that the firm's participative rhetoric disguises a 'stifling paternalism' and 'pseudo democracy'.

There are employers who make little pretence about their antipathy towards unions. Wal-Mart is one. Commercially it is a highly successful company, yet it has earned the dubious distinction of regularly upsetting its employees, provoking spiky websites such as *WallmartSucks.com*. There, aggrieved staff can vent their ire, such as

> Wal-Mart couldn't care less about anything. I went on leave to have a baby. Yes, I was gone 5 months. After I had the baby, I had my gall bladder out. Not to say that, three days after the baby came, my grandma passed away. When I called to tell them, the person that answered the phone couldn't care less. They said, 'aren't you on leave anyway?' Well, when I came back a few weeks ago, the team manager tells me they have to cut my pay because I was a supervisor in the deli and they had to replace me. Now they only have part-time openings.

The extent to which unions positively or negatively affect the labour market is much debated. The relationship is complicated by variations in the functions of particular unions, differences in union law, and whether union membership is compulsory or voluntary. Prime Minister Margaret Thatcher outlawed the union 'closed shop'—only union members could be hired—in the UK in 1993, followed by a similar move in Australia. Elsewhere where there is blanket prohibition, it is not always enforced or is worked around, such as in the entertainment and the construction sectors in the USA (where the closed shop was banned as early as 1947).

There are construction unions in the USA that run 'hiring halls', often with exclusive agreements with employers for all, or a fixed percentage of, workers to be from the union.

Adherents to unfettered capitalism—which has not had the best of records in recent years—regard unions as obstructions to economic growth. They claim that they increase the wages of their members at the expense of available jobs. Unions, they assert, are anachronisms, ill suited to late-modern organizational and working patterns and often unnecessarily prolonging disputes. In the partisan, often heated, discussions over the role of unions, arguments can be mustered to support either side. What does seem clear is that the traditional role of the union in protecting employee rights is diluted when there is robust legal protection for workers and enlightened human resource management. On the other hand, there are many situations that do not fit this picture, and unions can be the only meaningful voice for oppressed or insecure groups of workers. Under these circumstances, it is union organization and power that can press for change, directly with specific employers, or more broadly on the political stage where Industrial Regulation is fashioned.

Chapter 3
Working a career

You read many times (in the past) that once you were hired
into an organization you would be there from cradle to grave
and never have to worry. I think that today people have
careers, but build on these careers by taking their knowledge
from company to company in search of the golden ring.

There is no such thing as a secure job anymore. It seems like
at any second someone can be on the streets looking for a
new job either voluntarily or involuntarily. I am so
frightened to not find a job...with the high expectations
I have set myself, failure is not an option.

These are the voices of young people about to start their working
life. They may be a tad nostalgic, but they are a contrast to those
of a previous generation when access to work was generally more
straightforward. It was an era when loyalty to an employer—
'delivering the goods' and 'keeping your nose clean'—was rewarded
with security and, for some, promotion. William Hollingsworth
Whyte captured the ethos well in his 1950s book *The
Organization Man*. He charted the progress of young recruits to
the corporate world who willingly gave over themselves, and the
control of their future, to the organization: 'They have an implicit
faith that The Organization will be interested in making use of
their best qualities as they are themselves, and thus, with

equanimity, they can entrust the resolution of their destiny to The Organization.' The sons and daughters of Organization Man face a rather different future, to quizzically reflect on his metaphors of progress: 'climbing the ladder', 'working your way through the ranks', 'moving up the hierarchy'.

The shape and availability of careers may have changed, but the notion that we will have a pathway of work experiences over a substantial proportion of our lifetime remains a robust cultural norm—if harder to realize. A career can be defined by a single occupation over a working lifetime—doctor, dentist, actor, plumber, bricklayer, train driver. Alternatively, it may be a series of different, disconnected, occupations or jobs. Criteria of good and less-good careers mirror the prevailing social climate, such as the value placed on service to the community, on security, status, pay, prospects, personal satisfaction—or greed. Some careers change radically in appeal with the times, like the decline in ecumenical careers at the end of the twentieth century. In the 1980s, careers in law and management consultancy were amongst the most popular, to be edged out in the 1990s by financial services and green/environmental jobs. In the early 2000s, careers in systems and software engineering were particular favourites.

Children are exposed to career language at an early age. There are primary schools that instruct their young charges on the structure and presentation of a good CV and what represent sensible career aspirations (deflating aspirations to be an astronaut, pop star, or sports hero). Focus is on 'what employers look for' and pragmatic advice drawn from the adult world they have yet to join. These initiatives hover between sensibly laying the foundations for full citizenship, and a premature takeover of the child's playfulness and identity. Despite such efforts, there are still many young people who reach early adulthood with little conception of what they want to do, or what they can do. Moreover, career pathways are rarely evenly distributed: class, race, and education readily open or close opportunities, and some choices are linked to long-standing gendered beliefs—the 'suitable' careers for men or women.

The demise of the linear career

The traditional, linear, career—blue collar and white collar—was constructed around menwho grew up during the Second World War. Getting a job and starting a career soon after schooling were prerequisites for marriage and starting a family, 'setting down'. Wives would give up their jobs to devote their energies to homemaking, motherhood, and accommodating their husband's career. Women who played a productive part in factory work during the war lost their jobs to returning men after the war, and were expected to resume their pre-war domestic roles. Any stresses of work and marriage were usually carefully contained and well camouflaged, while dependence on a male breadwinner militated against divorce.

Today, societal transformation has impinged on all facets of this career model. There are delays in the transition from school to work. There are many more women in the workforce. Child rearing is no longer exclusively female or incompatible with working. Working long hours is commonplace, as is long-distance commuting and moving home. There are often explicit tensions in managing the boundaries between careers and other spheres of life, especially domestic, child care, and leisure. In sum, careers have become more complex—and more fragile. The best-laid plans can be derailed by redundancy, recession, divorce, or illness, as well as serendipity—those chance ocurrences and opportunities. Michael Apted's *Seven Up* documentary was replete with such instances. His unusual television series tracked fourteen British schoolchildren from the age of seven in 1964, then every seven years up to *56 Up* in 2012. For example:

> Tony at 7 wanted to be a jockey. He realized his dream by 21, but then gave it up for life as a London taxi driver. His ambitions then

switched to acting, which put his marriage under strain, and he confessed to adultery. By 49 he was a well-off man with three homes.

Neil was an exuberant, hopeful 7-year-old, but dropped out of university at 21, homeless and struggling to cope. By 35, he was writing and doing some local acting. By 42, he had found a supportive partner. In 49 UP he had become a political candidate, standing in the 2010 general election—but was unsuccessful.

Jackie and Lynne were London working-class girls both from the same primary school. Jackie went on to attend a comprehensive secondary school, Lynne a grammar school. Both were married by their early twenties, but thereafter their paths diverged. Jackie had several jobs, got divorced, and became a single parent. Lynne started a career in librarianship at 21 and stuck with it.

Charles was from the wealthy London area of Kensington and at 7 already had his eye on a place at Oxford or Cambridge after his public school education. Things did not go quite to plan as he failed Oxford entrance examinations, but he gained a place at Durham University instead. He attended Oxford later, as a post-graduate. His career then developed rapidly in journalism, including producing documentary films for the BBC.

A boundaryless career?

The idea of a boundaryless career was first mooted in the early 1990s by American management academic Michael Arthur. He claimed that traditional careers, which were mostly confined to a single-employment setting, were fast disappearing. In their place were boundaryless careers, spanning many employers and workplaces, involving different occupations and switches between job roles.

Boundaryless careers were a result of an increasingly competitive global marketplace: few organizations could continue to operate as they once did. To survive, many needed to restructure or downsize. Back-up services that were once part of the organization's in-house workforce were now outsourced, sometimes abroad, aided by virtual technologies. Where promotion was once through the ranks, many of these ranks were vanishing as organizations strove to become 'leaner and fitter'. And where long-term contracts of employment were once the norm, they had now become a handicap to an employer seeking to minimize the salary bill and overheads. The predictable, linear, career was in its death throes.

Some of the main distinctions between boundaryless and traditional careers are summarized in Figure 4.

	Traditional	Boundaryless
Employment relationship:	Job security for loyalty	Employability for performance and flexibility
Boundaries:	One or two firms	Multiple firms
Skills:	Firm specific	Transferable
Success measured by:	Pay, promotion, status	Different roles and occupations, intrinsic rewards
Responsibility for career:	Organization	Individual
Milestones:	Age-related	Learning-related

4. Contrasting traditional and boundaryless careers

A career without boundaries requires boundaryless people, prepared to be flexible, mobile, and inventive—or protean (after the Greek god Proteus, noted for his ability to rapidly assume different forms). Protean workers are in charge of their own career, no longer dependent on the organization to shape their future. They anticipate and adapt to shifts in the labour market and different organizational demands. They do not expect an off-the-shelf career identity, but craft it through their own employability—cultivating transferable skills to work effectively in different and unfamiliar contexts. The foundations of this mind-set are to be laid down in school and university, supported by 'lifelong' training and learning opportunities.

The demise of loyalty

Strong allegiance to a single employer, or to very few employers, has been a cornerstone of the traditional career. The boundaryless career is different. Workers no longer expect to be in the same organization for many years, and certainly not for their whole career. Loyalty's unquestioned goodness—ethically and economically—is substantially challenged.

Shrinking loyalty raises questions about the very viability of an organization when its members are regularly contemplating the next move, looking over their shoulders for jobs elsewhere. But if a traditional organization can ossify because of lack of movement and renewal, a boundaryless one faces the opposite problem: potentially too loose to cohere. The trick is in achieving a managed balance. The individual needs to protect their own career flexibility but, at the same time, the employer needs a degree of workforce stability. It is in the employer's interest to retain people who possess skills essential to the organization's core activities— assets readily squandered in times of rapid worker turnover and organizational restructuring. Hence, supporting core workers with longer-term contracts and development opportunities should be mutually advantageous—and also ripe for idiosyncratic deals.

Idiosyncratic deals are the very opposite of collectively set, or bureaucratically determined, working terms and conditions (such as on the basis of age, experience, or seniority). Idiosyncratic deals include special salaries, desired work locations, travel benefits, and family-friendly working hours. They can be found in a wide range of employment sectors, such as the media, academia, finance, IT, small firms, and start-ups. Idiosyncratic deals are normally confidential, providing core workers with working conditions that are especially meaningful to them, but without an obligation on the employer to deliver such benefits to everyone. And there is the rub: their secrecy can fuel suspicion amongst co-workers and open the door to nepotism and 'old boy' networks.

Contingent workers

Core workers help stabilize an organization, but not without the support of contingent workers. Contingent workers are hired in as and when necessary on temporary or part-time contracts, some 'just in time' for particular projects. The organization has no long-term commitments to these workers, such as regular salaries, insurance, or overheads. The contingent worker's role is purely transactional and their loyalty to their client temporary—not ideal for a relaxed relationship with core workers or their managers. The upsurge of contingent workers has given rise to a new management specialism, along with advice books on 'how to manage the contingent worker'.

Contingent workers are of two broad types. There are low-skilled service workers on casual contracts, such as for cleaning, security, clerical, and catering work. And there are highly skilled, specialized, knowledge workers, hired for their professional expertise in fields such as computing, production, software systems, market research, organizational development, and staff recruitment. Many contingent workers have made a protean shift, reinventing themselves after unemployment or redundancy. Some are individual freelancers, others are attached to companies that specialize in outsourced services.

The growth of the low-skilled, contingent, workforce has been a boon for contractors who specialize in recruiting and placing workers in temporary jobs. There are major companies that manage many thousands of contingent workers nationally and internationally. In processing and placing contingent workers, these enterprises often lack depth knowledge about the workers they sign up, about the jobs for which they are hiring, or about their client's workplaces. The stark picture is revealed in a major study by John Allen and Nick Henry. They describe contract service firms as hollow corporations made up of fragments, each contract site separate from the others and owned by a different employer.

Contingent workers are isolated from central operations and remote from other people on the client's site: 'you're on your own.'

Being a contingent worker is an uncertain business, seeking work in a competitive marketplace. But it is the low skilled who shoulder the weightiest burden. They are more exposed to periods without work, to poor pay, and lack benefits such as sick leave and unemployment insurance. They constitute a growing precariat— people who live precariously 'as normal'. And they are open to exploitation. In her book *Hard Work*, journalist Polly Toynbee describes the sense of insecurity and powerlessness of the low-status contingent worker. On one occasion she presented herself, identity disguised, to an agency that had advertised for a catering attendant. Her initial encounter ran as follows:

> I was nearly five minutes early…
> 'Who you for?' asked the surly security guard.
> 'Sally Hampton,' I said.
> 'She don't work here.'
> 'Yes she does. She called me for an interview today.'
> 'I SAID, she don't work here no more.'.....
> 'I've come miles to see her. I was told to see her. I want to see someone else. About the job that was advertised!'…
> 'Ain't nobody here. You mean a catering job?'
> 'Yes, in the Town Hall.'
> 'I don't know nothing about it. All I know is all yesterday and all today there were loads, I mean loads, of folks coming here for Sally Hampton and they all been sent away. She left, for good. No interviews today.'

Events like this expose the bleaker side of the boundaryless career. Those lacking 'career capital' are cheap labour and can be treated cheaply. Without the educational attainments, advanced skills, or domestic flexibility to join the protean elite, they have to seek work within the burgeoning ranks of the poorly paid, where insecurity is greatest and where obligation to the worker is, at best, cursory.

New careers, new constraints

The traditional career does resemble an endangered species on its way to extinction, but declining in a gradual and piecemeal way. Some organizations have yet to adjust to a highly competitive, information economy (a 'structural lag', in economists' jargon), while there are still individuals, especially older ones, wedded to the notion of a traditional career path. But as the traditional career fades, other models have emerged. They typically prioritize individual initiative, personal agility, and openness to rapid change and learning. New labels have been invented, such as the portfolio career, post-corporate career, intelligent career, and responsible career.

The portfolio genre, for example, invites individuals to contract out their skills to a variety of different employers or clients, and construct a mix of work activities—a portfolio of various income streams and challenges. The portfolio was originally advocated in the early 1990s by business writer and management consultant Charles Handy. He explained that 'portfolio people' were 'the sort of people who, when you ask them what they do, reply, "It will take a while to tell you it all, which bit would you like?" Sooner or later we shall all be portfolio people. It is good news.' A multi-stranded portfolio would be a hedge against the risks inherent in the single-job career and could comprise, for instance, paid work, domestic work in one's own home, gift work (voluntary community work), and study work (reading, studying for a new skill or qualification).

Handy's enthusiasm for portfolios was acted out in his own, professional, lifestyle—as a well-off man with established employment networks. But his sunny prescriptions gloss over the effort and stress of sustaining a portfolio, especially when one is not a member of the professional elite. As one portfolioer confesses, it entails 'exhausting labour of creating and sustaining a presence, continually assessing boundaries, pleasing unpredictable clients, contract juggling and worrying about unpredictable income'. A portfolio requires constant attention, and can be challenging for people new to entrepreneurial activity. It can be even more fraught when income-generation opportunities are scarce, and when home and family demands spill over or intrude. Having been made redundant, there are portfolio workers who find themselves competing with ex-colleagues for pieces of work from their previous employer, 'crumbs from the table', as their search for *any* paid work becomes an abiding preoccupation.

The flexible organization

Flexible careers and flexible organizations are two sides of the same coin. A flexible organization offers adaptability on the hours an employee can work, the place where they can work, the structure of their work role, and the support for their family responsibilities. Some of the possibilities are summarized in Figure 5.

Time	Place	Structure	Support
Flexitime	Working from home	Job-sharing	Parental leave
Staggered hours	Teleworking		Workplace nursery
Annualized hours			
Self-rostering			
Term-time working			
Compressed hours			

5. The flexible organization

Various permutations of working hours have now become common: the 9 to 5 day is no longer the only way. Hours can be staggered or compressed to suit individual circumstances. Being physically present 'at work' is no longer essential for many jobs, creating opportunities to work remotely, such as from home. This can increase a worker's availability, reduce the hassle of commuting, and save the organization the costs of office and equipment space. Job sharing is more convenient for people with young children and other dependents. And paid leave can provide a welcome break for new parents at crucial periods of their lives.

The motives for introducing flexible practices vary. Some arise from employee pressure; others from shortages of key staff; and still others from changes in the flow of production or services. Indeed, 'flexible for whom?' is a fair question to pose to an organization that is considering flexible working practices. When a particular version of flexibility is pressed upon existing staff by an employer, it starts on a very different footing from mutually negotiated, or employee-requested, flexibility. Moreover, certain flexible practices, such as compressed working hours, can be a mixed blessing—freeing-up workers' time, but simultaneously intensifying their work and raising stress levels. The following are cases in point:

Redditch Council gardeners had a heavy workload in summer and contractors had to be bought in to help out. In winter, though, the gardeners were considerably underemployed. Annualized hours were seen to be the solution. It meant a four-day week in winter but with no loss of earnings, and longer hours in summer. The savings from the contractors' budget created more jobs and there was no overall loss of earning over the year. The workers' response? 'The men were up in arms at the start. But being honest, if you tried to take it off them now they'd commit murder. Most have got small children and enjoy having time off over the Christmas holiday to spend with their family.'

Playtex wanted to introduce flexitime for their 450 production employees and 150 office staff. Following a joint union/ management survey, it was agreed to implement a 38 hour week over four days, with Friday to Sunday off. Full-time hours were 7.45 am to 5.45 pm with 30 minutes break. The workers' response? 'The system works well and is very popular now. Even though some people find the longer days tiring, they love having the long weekends every week. There's certainly no wish to go back. Productivity has improved.'

KPMG faced the prospect of large scale redundancies because of recessionary pressures. Under the banner of 'Flexible Futures' they sought to minimize job losses and retain their talented staff. Staff could reduce their working week by an unpaid day and/or take sabbatical leave of four-to-twelve weeks at 30 per cent of pay. The workers' response? 'Just the fact that we were clearly trying to do something different created a great feeling of "all for one"; 85 per cent of staff signed up for the scheme.'

Many job applicants now request flexibility, and flexible working has become a strategic objective for a growing number of organizations. But employer conversion is far from universal. Some react nervously, fearing less commitment from their workers (despite considerable evidence to the contrary). For many smaller organizations, flexibility is synonymous with discontinuity and disruption—something that they feel they cannot absorb.

There are very few organizations that offer choices across the whole of the flexibility spectrum, but those that do are exemplars of what can be achieved. Ikea is a case in point, roundly embracing the philosophy by, in effect, offering idiosyncratic deals to all—as evidenced by one of its Netherlands' advertisements:

Time has gone when 'the boss' decides how your workday is organized. Everybody chooses the job that fits him or her. Even better: compose your job yourself. We make individual arrangements over working hours (varying from six to 36 hours, different parts of the day, evenings, weekends), career development, job content, education etc. We offer options at every level, in different areas, inside and outside the subsidiary, inside and outside the Netherlands.

Ikea's thinking is essentially pragmatic. In the words of their UK Human Relations manager: 'As long as it works for the business, they have the freedom to work flexibly.'

Chapter 4
Men's work, women's work

The Industrial Revolution triggered a reshaping of the sexual demographics of the workplace. In the physically lighter trades, women were a cheaper and more flexible option than men, valued for their 'natural', home-honed skills of fine hand-work, well suited to textile, pottery, and clothing manufacture. The emerging industries also provided women with an alternative to domestic service (or the black economy of sweatshops and prostitution). Most women, nevertheless, regarded their paid work as a secondary identity, their primary one being in the . home, as a wife and mother. As the machineries of the Industrial Revolution became heavier and more complex— steelmaking, mining, ship building—men were to dominate most rank-and-file jobs, as well as prime positions of supervision and control.

By the mid-nineteenth century, these structural changes interlaced with the gender and sexual politics of the times, in particular the prudishness of Victorian Britain. It was an era when human sexuality was veiled in euphemism or totally repressed. In polite company, sexual topics were not to be discussed. A sexually mixed workforce could, therefore, endanger the moral order, so it was often important to keep the sexes apart. There were managers in the emerging industries who feared that their male workers, especially, would be deflected from their productive endeavours in the presence of the opposite sex. They might well engage in 'distractive behaviours', such as chatting, flirting, and courting.

On occasions, addressing the potential problem could take a farcical turn, such as the early years of the British Foreign Office in London. Female typists were quietly relegated to an isolated attic, far from the working hubbub of the male clerks. The only indication that the attic was occupied was a discreet arrow on the staircase labelled 'To the Typewriters'. The separation of the sexes was put to the test when payday came. To collect their pay, the women had to go to the cashier's office on the ground floor, thereby mixing with men in the corridors. The managers' solution was to evacuate the corridors and shut all the office doors while the women rushed to get their money, then scurried back to their attic bolthole.

By the early twentieth century, the male boss and breadwinner had become a common feature of modernization, as well as work that was deemed dominantly male or female. The all-female typing pool and men forging heavy steel chains were emblematic of the times (see Figure 6 and 7).

Segregation today

Today, in the West, sexual probity is rarely a reason to separate men from women in the workplace, although in other regions of the globe this is not necessarily the case. In Muslim countries, for example, where purdah is practised, women are excluded from most work where men are present and, in its strictest form, from all activity in the labour market. Traditionally, purdah has been presented as a way of protecting women and respecting their modesty (where the burka screens their body from public gaze). But to a liberal Western eye it can appear anachronistic, a practice

6. **Women's work in the early twentieth century**

that keeps women in a subservient role and unable to interact with men on an equal footing.

The religious/social customs of Saudi Arabia are illustrative. Women can work only with the permission of their male guardian but, when men and women do work in the same company, there are strict rules to keep them apart. Work premises typically have separate staff entrances, as well as divided sections for customers—such as McDonald's in Riyadh which has one area for bachelors and another for women and couples with children. Except for a few women-only restaurants, women are banned from waitressing. Control in Saudi society is exercised through a

7. Men's work in the early twentieth century

combination of a powerful religious orthodoxy, and a wealthy, male, autocracy—the Saudi family. Together they have resisted significant changes to male privilege. On returning to work in her father's jewellery shop in Jeddah, one of my own students, now familiar with Westernized customer service, was obliged to withdraw to a backroom each time a male customer entered the shop. 'I'm now rather confused about all this', she confessed.

The jobs' divide

Sex segregation may not be part of everyday life in the West, but major sectors of the job market are informally divided by gender, both horizontally (between different occupations) and vertically (between different levels of an occupation). Figure 8 shows some of the most divided occupations in the USA.

Generally, women are more prevalent in the personal and caring services, work requiring face-to-face interactions with customers or clients—especially in health, social work, and education. In the UK, over 40 per cent of these jobs are in the public sector. Men, on the other hand, are more likely to be found in jobs that relate to

Dominantly Male Jobs	Dominantly Female Jobs
95% +	**90% +**
Scaffolder/rigger	Childcare worker
Train driver	Hairdresser
Crane operator	Occupational therapist
Car mechanic	Nurse
Electrician	Primary/nursery teacher
Plumber	Domestic cleaner
Pilot	
Firefighter	**80–85%**
Mechanical Engineer	Clerk/receptionist
Heavy goods/truck driver	Librarian
	Social worker
80–85%	Travel agent
Production manager	
Police supervisor	**66–73%**
Software developer	Office administrator
Security guard	Human resource manager
	Social services manager
75–79%	Counsellor
Architect	Customer service
Corporate CEO	Catering assistant

8. **Different jobs for different genders**

'things' or physical strength, such as construction, transport, engineering, or security. Vertical divisions reflect gender biases (intentional or otherwise) in decisions on recruitment and promotion, resulting in fewer women at higher levels of management and the professions. Men have long held the vast majority of top positions in major corporations and, at the current rate of change, the estimate is that it will take at least another fifty years before parity is achieved.

From their early years, children's attitudes towards occupations begin to reflect gender socialization. They reproduce the view that many women's jobs are less 'cool' or less important. Young schoolchildren are soon able to split jobs into male (lorry driver, engineer, soldier, computer programmer, plumber, farmer), and female (nurse, care assistant, primary school teacher, fashion designer, secretary, librarian), and frame their personal job choices around gender stereotypes: 'women are more caring and better at talking to people'; 'men are stronger'. Some of these attitudes cross the generations, while others shift as children are exposed to different role models at home and in the media. There are, for example, a number of traditionally male occupations that children now no longer see exclusively in that way, such as police officers, managers, lawyers, doctors, cooks, bakers, postal workers, and social workers.

Feminist pressure on working conditions has led to a general increase in the proportion of women employed, as well as to the prohibition of sexual discrimination in the workplace. The effects, though, are uneven. For example, in 2008 there was an average of 72 per cent of women in employment in Denmark, Sweden, and the Netherlands. In contrast, Italy, Hungary, and Malta had only 45 per cent. One of the most common gender splits is in part-time employment: women are far more likely to be found in part-time work than men. In 2010, nearly 33 per cent of women in the EU were employed on a part-time basis, compared to 9 per cent of men. The Netherlands had the highest proportion of women in part-time work—over 75 per cent. According to British sociologist Catherine Hakim, a reason for this pattern is that women themselves are far from unanimous in their preference for a work-centred lifestyle (a factor, she contends, that outweighs any discriminatory forces). She suggests that most women willingly choose flexible, part-time, work because they want to combine work and family. The remainder are evenly split—between childless women who are heavily invested in qualifications and training for work, and those focused solely on their family and children.

The pay divide

Wherever a women stands on her desire for paid work—as a committed careerist or for a mixed work/family portfolio—it is a stark fact that her pay is likely to be less than a man's. It exists when 'male' and 'female' jobs are compared, and also when men and women are doing identical work. The gap persists regardless of qualifications, fuelling the popular belief that 'women have to be twice as good as men to keep up'. For the relatively few women who reach top executive positions, their salaries and performance bonuses are mostly inferior to those of men. Women's bonuses tend to remain flat regardless of company performance, while men in top leadership positions enjoy increased bonuses. Flexible jobs that are 'female' are amongst the poorest paid of all jobs, and it not uncommon for a woman to incur a financial penalty when she temporally breaks employment to have children or undertake other caring roles.

The global picture of median male/female pay differentials is shown in Figure 9. Across twenty-two countries men consistently win out on pay, but with some marked variations in how much. A female worker in Korea or Japan earns over a third less than an equivalent man, but in Belgium, New Zealand, Poland, and Denmark the gap falls to around 10 per cent. The UK ranks towards the higher end of the earning gap, a discordant note for a nation that professes (and legislates for) sexual equality.

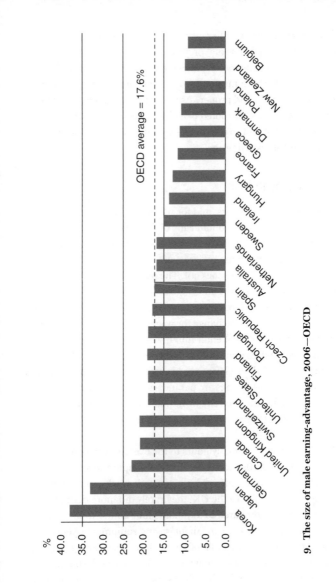

9. The size of male earning-advantage, 2006—OECD

The variations reflect different cultural histories, gender ideologies, as well as sexual prejudices. In cultures where male dominance is firmly rooted and widely accepted, it is not uncommon for both men and women to embrace inequality in earnings as 'right and proper'. As with most employment matters, pay can reflect deeply rooted beliefs and dogmas on gender and power. It is prudent to judge any inequalities—at least initially—in their own contextual terms.

On the home front

Who does the housework, and for whom, has long been gendered—as well as economically divided. For instance, a woman who is employed to do someone's housework counts formally towards a nation's economic prosperity; the same work given freely in her own home does not. The point was elegantly made nearly a century ago by Cambridge economist Arthur Pigou: '…the services rendered by women enter into the dividend when they are rendered in exchange for wages, whether in the factory or in the home, but do not enter into it when they are rendered by mothers and wives gratuitously to their own families. Thus, if a man marries his housekeeper or his cook, the national dividend is diminished. These things are paradoxes.' Pigou captured well the modern predilection to reify work that involves a financial exchange, but to ignore or devalue work that does not.

Housework can add many hours to the overall workload of a family. In the 1940s the gender line was simply and sharply drawn: men performed very little domestic work—save some fixing and building. In the UK, they rarely did more than fifteen minutes a day, compared to a woman's four hours. Today, the gap is much less (in part due to labour-saving equipment), yet women continue to take on the bulk of the washing up, cleaning, tidying, and washing of clothes (some fourteen hours a week compared to men's five hours). And unlike the 1940s, it is done at irregular or unsocial hours, after full- or part-time work. In total, women in the UK do nine hours a week on chores, equivalent to an extra day's work. A similar pattern has been observed in the USA. It is more exaggerated in countries such as Greece, Turkey, and Portugal where women, as traditional homemakers, expect—and are expected—to undertake the major proportion of housework. In contrast, Scandinavian egalitarianism shows up in a fairly even sharing of household chores.

Some commentators argue that unequal divisions of household chores are basically a matter of who has most spare time. Because of contrasting patterns of work, on average a woman is likely to be left with more spare time to do the housework. It is not an issue of gender roles. This explanation, however, is a little too pat. When men do have more spare time than women, especially if unemployed, they do not necessarily regard it as spare for household chores. And it is not uncommon for women who work longer hours than their partners, and earn more money, to still undertake the lion's share of housework. Some do so grudgingly, but others are less fussed. The woman remains the homemaker, while her partner—in collusion—continues to be treated as provider and controller of major decisions. Beth, a working wife in London, explains:

> My husband rarely volunteers to do anything; left to his own devices, he'd surf the net or fall asleep in front of the TV. He just doesn't 'see' mess or dirt, but he'll always do something if I nudge him, so I can't complain. I'm basically 'housework supervisor' while chipping in myself; I work considerably longer hours than him (and yes I'm one of those who earns more, but it all goes into the household pot). It works for us after 10 years of marriage. It's just housework—100 years from now it's not going to matter if the carpets were clean or the sink needed scrubbing.

New man, new arrangements?

The 1980s heralded the maturing of 'new man' in the USA and UK. New man took a major role in domestic activities, rejected sexist attitudes, and was sensitive and caring. New man contrasted with 'old', macho man, a product of traditional, working-class upbringing; a person who was distant from his children and often denigrating of women. New man was different—educated, middle class, and egalitarian.

Today, the spirit of new man is alive and well in some families. There are partners who have renegotiated their household and caring roles, men readily re-balancing or reversing the traditional structure (he is now full- or part-time carer and household manager). But the hard data suggests that transformations of this sort have been patchy and, overall, new man has stalled in his domestic tracks. Women's employment has resulted in only a modest increase in their control over family decision-making and finances, and they continue to shoulder a disproportionate burden of childcare and domestic labour and, as the above discussion suggests, not always reluctantly.

Crossing over

Crossing the gender divide in jobs has tended to favour men; they have been more successful than women in breaking down traditional divisions. Impelled by the decline in white collar and manufacturing jobs, men have migrated to traditionally female jobs, such as nursing, librarianship, primary school teaching, and flight cabin crew. Given prevailing gender stereotypes, these transitions have not always been easy, but they compare favourably to women trying to enter long-established male domains—such as construction, firefighting, and engineering.

Construction has been typically a culturally closed world of male prerogative, where women workers can be objectified and harassed. Accounts from women on construction teams reveal how threatened men feel by their presence. Some are denied key information, or given the wrong tools; others are more directly undermined: 'A woman described how, on her first day on the job at a construction site, the foreman said, "I never worked with no fucking women and I ain't never going to. I will run you off of this job before the week is over".'

The firefighting service has, also, not exactly been welcoming to women. The few women who have managed to secure front-line firefighting jobs have had to deal with in-house discrimination— including sexual harassment, male derision, and poorly fitting equipment—before they can deal with actual fires. To the charge that firefighting is physically beyond them, they can point to the fact that technique is often more important than brute strength, and that women played essential firefighting roles during the Second World War in the UK and the USA: they stood in for firemen who had been conscripted into the military. Looking further back in time, as early as 1878 the then all-women Girton College in Cambridge formed its own fire brigade under the tutelage of the captain of London Fire Brigade (Figure 10). It followed a too-close-for-comfort conflagration of nearby haystacks, for which the College had no defences. Significantly, it

10. The Girton fire brigade, 1878

took more than another 100 years before the London Fire Brigade recruited its first female operational firefighter, and today there are less than 4 per cent of women firefighters in the UK. The USA does only slightly better at 4.5 per cent. In 2010, New York City had a total of 11,500 firefighters: just 31 were women.

Despite the efforts of engineering unions and educators to attract more women into the engineering profession, male dominance prevails. The feminization of engineering has been slow and irregular in Western countries. In the UK, fewer than 7 per cent of professional engineers are women. The USA and France have exceeded this at respectively 12 per cent and 27 per cent. Yet all are overshadowed by Russia and China, where gender diversity in engineering has been a historical feature of state education and employment. In the former USSR, women comprised nearly 60 per cent of the engineering workforce. It declined with the collapse of the USSR, but still remains relatively high at around 40 per cent—a similar figure to China.

The tools and technologies of engineering symbolize masculinity, an image that has had a potent influence on the public perception of the industry. A woman in the West who wants to study engineering will typically join a higher education programme where the majority of students and staff are men, and its subculture distinctly masculine. For these reasons alone, many women disqualify themselves; they feel uncomfortable, out of place, even though their entry qualifications can be more than sufficient.

When in post, women deal with the male culture in different ways. Some put their faith in being good, capable, engineers: 'Once I'd proved that I was there to get on with it, I think that kind of barrier just went.' Others prefer to adopt 'male' norms of self-promotion and claim their place as 'one of the boys': 'I give them as good as I get. So it's equal. And you have to laugh. If you give them respect, you'll get respect back.' In these ways, gender becomes a malleable social resource to renegotiate for instrumental ends. But not all women adapt. Some find the male ethos oppressive. They speak of feeling insecure in the face of discrimination—stereotyped or ignored, and given less responsibility than their male colleagues.

Glass ceilings, walls, and escalators

In the early 1970s, two American psychologists, Kay Deaux and Tim Emswiller, conducted an intriguing experiment. They asked a mixed-sex group of people to individually rate how some men and women perform on a series of tasks, and to say how much of their performance was due to ability or luck. The tasks were rigged to be stereotypically male (e.g. involving a tyre jack or a wrench) or female (some common household objects). They found that effective performance by man on a masculine task was more often attributed to skill, whereas identical performance by a female on the same task was considered to be more influenced by luck. In the words of the researchers, 'what is skill for the male is luck for the female'. Stereotypical attributions of this sort plague women as they attempt to move on and up in organizations, and where progress is defined by male criteria of success.

In many countries, equal opportunities legislation has ensured that sex discrimination plays no official part in organizational practices. Regulation has curbed obvious prejudice—such as recruitment drives that specify the sex or age of eligible applicants. There are now both voluntary and mandatory targets that add impetus to gender-balanced workforces. But less-visible barriers persist, such as workplace cultures that privilege aggressiveness, forcefulness, and decisiveness in men, but not women. Phrases such as 'he's incisive, she's abrasive', 'he's busy, she has trouble with deadlines'; 'he's thoughtful; she's hesitant'; 'he's prudent, she's passive', add to the marginalization of women.

The gendering of an organization's culture mirrors the attitudes of the people in charge. Men who hold senior positions can consciously or unconsciously perpetuate a 'male' outlook—because of who they are and because of their positions of control. And there is also the lure of the 'old school tie', preferring job applicants who are 'like me/us' and 'will blend in'. In combination, these processes can perpetuate existing, dominant, interests. The feminist challenge here is straightforward: the more an organization is dominated and controlled by men, the less likely it is that women will have a significant voice. It does not preclude women's influence and options, but it stacks the odds against them.

The cumulative effect is obstructed progress. Many women report that they know that they are hitting barriers, being impeded or bypassed at work, but find it hard to 'prove' or pinpoint exactly why. They meet glass walls and glass ceilings. Men, in contrast, appear to glide by on glass escalators—a smoother passage to promotion. It is instructive, then, to cast a quizzical eye over the much-vaunted *Fortune 500* companies—the 500 most profitable US industrial corporations, annually compiled by the aptly titled *Fortune* magazine. In 2010, only fifteen were run by women, and women held just 10 per cent of senior management posts overall. The picture is replicated in many national governments. In the UK, privately educated Oxbridge men, of wealthy background and 'good connections', have long dominated the ruling political elite.

Women at the top

Women in the boardroom have the potential to influence matters. Their presence can increase the diversity of views and help counteract groupthink: the tendency of an executive board to reach consensus without critically evaluating their ideas. In this manner mixed boards should be better able to appraise any risks facing the business. And indeed, there are now a few studies that put some hard data to this expectation. They suggest that companies with a higher proportion of women on senior management teams often have healthier sales and stronger stock-market performance than their rivals.

Historically, the inclusion of women at the top of organizations has proceeded at a snail's pace, even amongst the most egalitarian of nations. The proportion of company directors who are women ranges from under 1 per cent in Japan, to over 35 per cent in Norway. In the UK it is 8 per cent and USA 11 per cent. Countries such as Sweden, Norway, Iceland, and Spain have forced matters, boosting female representation by positive discrimination—legally requiring firms to have a minimum quota of women on their board. In Norway, the first country to do this, the target quota is 40 per cent. It is not uncommon, nevertheless, for women to feel as if they are a token presence. One describes her early experience:

> I was the only female on my first Board and that took some getting used to all around. It was also an international Board of various cultures. The most important guidance I can give to others is to be yourself. Don't behave how you think people expect you too— sometimes I have observed women 'copying' poor male behavior because it is 'expected'. By staying true to what you do and how you do it is really important.

> I had a disagreement with a Chairman on a specific topic which centred around my area of expertise. Although we resolved it well, he initially reverted to what others would refer to as 'sexist comments' but not what I considered to be of a personally offensive nature. His 'quips' really didn't bother me as having an engineering background, I have thick skin, but others were trying to convince me to take action. I did think about it, I spoke directly to him and we resolved it, but it was an example of my dealing with the situation in my way, not as others thought I should.

Such independence of mind has intrigued psychologists, curious as to how minority female directors carve their niche on mixed-sex boards. A Swedish study of a large number of company boards gives us some clues. The researchers found that women directors who had fought their way to the top (that is, not appointed automatically on a quota basis) displayed consistently different value preferences from their male colleagues. While male directors stressed power and achievement, the women pressed for novelty, excitement, and non-conformity. The female directors were less risk-averse than their male associates and contributed to some of the best of corporate decisions.

Dismantling gender barriers

The story of sexual inequality in the workplace is, as we have seen, about the opportunities and rewards that favour men, and the underlying prejudices. One approach to improve the situation has been to focus on a woman's personal character, strategies, and political skills. Women who wish to surmount gender barriers should, some experts advise, aim to be strikingly competent by 'consistently exceeding expectations', but not to the extent that their male colleagues feel too threatened. They should, additionally, seek highly visible assignments and locate influential mentors.

Though it is doubtful that success can be reduced to a particular stratagem, a combination of tenacity, tact, and obvious expertise has certainly helped high-achieving women steer a judicious path around the many barriers they have faced. We are, however, still left with the barriers. An exclusive focus on the individual amounts to blaming the victim for their circumstances and ignoring the structures and cultures that nourish male patronage. Opinions divide on how best to deal with them. Some argue that compulsion is the only way: it can kick-start change that otherwise would not happen and create a catalyst for transformation. The law has a role in specifying the minimum proportion of female representation on boards and outlawing sexual discrimination in the workplace. Shareholders can help by pressing for gender-fair polices in the organizations in which they have invested.

But others point to the drawbacks of such measures. Pushing hard often produces resentful compliance, tokenism, and evasion. Shareholding conglomerates (themselves often male-dominated) are likely to be more interested in the financial returns of their portfolio than its gender balance. A preferable approach would be to build positive change voluntarily and participatively from within the organization and its leadership, aiming for a succession of small gender-wins that, over time, will shift the culture of the organization. A gender-sensitive human resources policy could include diversity-awareness training, women's networks, flexible working practices, childcare services for women and men, business plans that incorporate women's voices, and special taskforces to address issues important to women.

Given that employers vary considerably in their appreciation of gender barriers, it is likely that both measures, external and internal, are necessary. But the exact mix would depend on prevailing gender norms and the extent of political consensus about 'the problem'. Meanwhile, there are women who cannot wait. They are impatient to escape the tangled web of corporate patriarchy and hierarchy; they choose to jump ship. Despite the financial challenges and high risks in starting a new business, a growing number of women have found this a welcome way out. They talk about the rewards that come from increased independence, from family flexibility, and from the greater opportunity to innovate. In the UK and USA, women-led firms have increased significantly in recent years and now make up some 30 per cent of the total self-employed.

Chapter 5
Struggling, surviving, thriving

> The tale is told of a management consultant hired to find ways
> of reducing the tedium of some assembly-line work. After
> observing one worker, a packer, doing the same task over and
> over again, he approached her and remarked: 'I've been
> watching you—that must be so boring, what you're doing.' The
> packer retorted, 'Not at all! Getting the different sizes just right
> in the boxes means I have to concentrate. And it feels good
> when I've got them all neatly stacked to be taken away.'

Central here is the notion of meaning: the human desire to make
meaning from what they do. A job that appears dreary and
monotonous to an outsider may, to the job holder, be experienced
differently. Or if not, there is the urge to self-justify by giving a
favourable impression to others. Where personal meaning cannot
be found, there is an emptiness that can grip workers of any skill
or level, at any period of their career.

Karl Marx regarded this as fundamentally an ideological problem.
The capitalist system, he argued, separated workers from their own
self-realization; they have lost control over their work and their
working conditions. Others—owners, executives—call the tune. As
a consequence, workers have become estranged from their core
'human nature'—to be free and productive in their own terms.

Pre-capitalist life was less shackled, a time when the worker—the butcher, the baker, the shoemaker, the candlestick maker—determined their own work schedules and content. For Marx, the capitalist worker is always alienated, disconnected from the means and objectives of production. It is an oppressive condition that can be relieved only when they regain control over what they produce and how they relate to one another. It follows that our packer lives in a bubble of delusion, captured and duped by the very system she serves, her consciousness systematically distorted.

This disconsolate image of industrial work was inspired by the 'dark satanic mills' of the Industrial Revolution. The productive miracle of mechanization was achieved on the back of the worker and the dehumanization of work—satirized by Charlie Chaplin in his iconic 1930s film *Modern Times*. Chaplin portrayed the worker as a cog in an unforgiving, ever-relentless, industrial machine. It was an era when time-and-motion experts were in much demand, prized for their skills in breaking down and measuring work for maximum efficiency, calculated in minutes and seconds. The technique formed a major part of 'scientific management' in the 1800s, the brainchild of engineer Frederic Winslow Taylor. Taylor became feted amongst management circles for his fastidious (and some would say obsessive) approach to speeding up production. His mission was to confront what he saw as endemic shirking ('soldiering') amongst production workers by eliminating all their 'wasteful actions', and controlling exactly how they performed their tasks.

The monumental assembly line of Henry Ford bore an uncanny resemblance to Taylor's methods. Inexpensive Model T cars were manufactured at record-breaking rates, rolling off the production line one every twenty-four seconds. Ford himself was known for his uncompromising autocracy and lack of empathy. When it was put to him that his factory work was soul destroying and dull, he responded with a curt denial: 'I have not been able to discover that repetitive labor injures a man in any way', he wrote. He added, for good measure, that his workers earned much higher wages than elsewhere, so they had little to complain about. And, to an extent, he was right, as there was no shortage of job applicants. Some workers could eventually afford to buy the very cars they produced—something of a public relations coup for Ford. Yet the reality was that working conditions were dire—relentlessly monotonous, dangerous, with suffocating fumes. Some people lost their lives. Getting through the very long day was a trial, eased only a little by drugs and alcohol taken before arriving at work, and during breaks in shifts.

By the late twentieth century, the nature and experience of work had been considerably reconfigured. In the West, the physical dangers were much reduced—and continue to be so—thanks to a raft of safety and health regulations. However, critics of the factory system have continued to point to the loss or absence of meaning for many workers, especially as craft skills have been replaced by automation and computerization. Global markets and mass production methods have reduced the role of traditional craft workers, such as bakers, brewers, shoemakers, printers, textile workers, metalworkers, pottery workers, and tailors. Once, for instance, a dressmaker undertook and owned the whole process, from selecting the material to designing, fitting, and making the garment. Now, other than high-end couture, she or he is more likely to be attending to a mere fragment of the product—a sleeve, a collar, some buttons—along a line of low-wage, 'flexible', workers with limited or zero prior experience of the trade. What used to require specialized training and long apprenticeship can now be performed by someone with little or no training. The work has become deskilled and the worker, in Karl Marx's terms, alienated.

A major casualty of deskilling is pride and dignity in one's work—a 'corrosion of character', in the words of sociologist Richard Sennett. Deskilling produces indifferent workers, people who have little stake in what they do. It is where, for example, a baker no longer has any physical contact with the contents or ingredients of bread making, other than through on-screen icons. The supermarket bakery-counter offers the impression and aroma of fresh baking, but there is little skill required in placing factory-prepared dough-mixes into a pre-programmed oven behind the counter. The baker does not actually know how to make bread; pushing buttons on a computerized machine is all that is required: 'Baking, shoemaking, printing, you name it, I've got the skills', mused one baker in Sennett's investigations. Deskilling applies to white collar workers too, such as teachers who complain of feeling deskilled when much of what and how they teach is determined by recipes and technologies handed down by government.

McJobs

The rationalization of work is epitomized by McJobs. 'McJob' is shorthand for low-skilled, low-status, dead-end work, a derivative of the McDonald's style of production and casual employment. McJobs are amongst the lowest paid, insecure, and are often taken by teenagers and minorities, mostly female. The 'McDonaldization' process is a highly efficient way of controlling the methods, quality, and quantity of work, a testimony to the legacy of Frederick Taylor and his 'scientific management'. It is where technology, rules, and tight management are closely harmonized.

McDonaldization extends well beyond fast food and flipping burgers. It can be found in businesses as varied as amusement parks, call centres, high-street retail chains, banks, hotels, and cash-and-carry warehouses. They share some or all of five ingredients: simple tasks; carefully time-controlled tasks that remove worker discretion and meaning; the same work hour after hour, day after day; computerized or robotized control over as many tasks as possible; and dehumanized work that results in rapid staff turnover. The level of external control means that there is little scope for personal initiative or creativity; employees are often scripted on what to say to customers. A recent exchange with a cashier in my local supermarket captures the ethos:

CASHIER: Thank you sir. Do you have a loyalty card?'
ME: 'Sure' (I point at the card that I'd already given him).
CASHIER (Wearily, and shifting into an unguarded moment): 'Sorry.
I'm just reading what I should say off the electronic till. It's like that in this job—a bit zombie-ish. I try to make each checkout a bit interesting and different, but it really can't be done. So easy to lose concentration.'

A key distinction between McJobs and other types of deskilled work is that McJobs require interaction with a customer or consumer—at best, ones who appreciate (or at least have learned to accept) the 'Mc' experience. The pervasiveness of McDonaldization has meant that many of us have become socialized into being McCustomers, expecting fast, predictable, unfussy service, with few frills or extended courtesies. But it can be a precarious encounter, where character corrosion spills over to the customer. There are, for instance, customers who feel free to abuse low-status, low-skilled workers when the service is not exactly as expected (in content, speed, language, or dialect), sheltering behind their 'sovereign consumer' position. Offshore call-centre operators are often the targets of personal insults and racist remarks—which they are taught to bear politely.

Inventing meaning

The image of the dehumanized workplace is a striking one. But there are ways in which we create meaning and purpose for ourselves, regardless of the formal nature of our work activities. Sub-cultures are central here: local, informal ways of working and meaning-making. They were first spotted by social scientists at Western Electric's Illinois plant, back in the 1920s. The investigators were struck by the fact that work groups on routine assembly tasks had their own notion of a fair day's work. It rarely corresponded to the one prescribed by management, but was carefully calibrated to avoid excessive or punitive action from management. The groups regulated their own pace and output, and devised their own means of correcting deviants. Individuals who worked too fast were openly accused of being 'rate busters', 'slaves', or 'speed kings', or were 'binged'—given a sharp blow to the upper arm. Those who worked too slowly also met with group disapproval, labelled 'chiselers'. In these various ways, much lively activity punctuated the monotony of their daily toil.

Humour

Meaning can be created through humour. Humour can be a counter or antidote to alienating work, helping to kill boredom. Jokes and laughter can bond colleagues and ease injuries to pride or dignity. Sharing a joke rich in irony can be a safe way to air feelings of hostility or contempt for a particular organizational policy, or a disliked manager or boss—a symbolic reset in the balance of power. In-group humour and gentle teasing can help restore feelings of control at work by establishing informal boundaries and norms, such as about who should run errands, what constitutes acceptable dress, and permissible sex talk. But humour also has a dark side. Sexist, racist, or homophobic jokes can undermine and humiliate colleagues. They can be especially hurtful when conformity pressures give cruel humour a false moral legitimacy: we laugh because others are laughing, not necessarily because we find the humour funny or acceptable.

Humour's remedial potential has not been lost on management experts, seeking ways to increase worker productivity. A small industry of 'fun and humour' consultants ('to help people get more smileage out of their lives and job') has arisen to advise companies on how humour can help relieve monotony and reduce stress. If the work itself is inherently taxing, then humour can be harnessed to make people feel easier and happier which will—they claim—lead to improved organizational effectiveness.

Organizations that have taken the fun message seriously have hired entertainers, dedicated specific work areas for play and games, and encouraged fun activities, such as 'silly hat' or 'dress down' days. These can be appreciated as welcome diversions, especially where long hours and repetitive tasks sap enthusiasm and dull concentration. As one worker observed, 'I worked at a company that had a ping pong table, large comfy sofas and chairs, a popcorn machine, small basketball hoop, etc in the break room. It was more like a mini community centre and it was great to see/meet co-workers who were in different departments and just take a healthy break.'

Fun activities like these are a balm or palliative for some of the dysfunctions of work. But closer analysis reveals that they should be applied with care—they can have unanticipated effects. In its 'natural' state, workplace fun is spontaneous and emergent, so when it is hired in or manufactured by an employer much of its impulsiveness and edge is lost. It can feel awkward and uncomfortable for some people; an unwanted imposition. An illustrative case is that of a British software firm. It gave its web-design department a 'fun makeover' to encourage 'new creative heights'. There were glass-walled offices and spaces redecorated in bright colours, all equipped like a child's play-room with toys and games. The centrepiece was a set of life-size Russian dolls to enliven the reception area, at a rumoured cost of £10,000—coinciding with strict budget cuts for the software staff.

The web designers did not react warmly to the initiative. They complained that they felt patronized by management and targeted the dolls to express their frustration. With subversive humour (not exactly the sort intended by management), they surreptitiously placed them in unusual, embarrassing, places—inside the elevator when clients were due to visit and in the ladies toilet. An angered management then installed a CCTV camera to watch the dolls, transforming their original project into serious farce. A moral of this tale is that the management appropriation of fun can be a risky venture if the politics and passions of employees are misread or overlooked.

Enriching work

There are ways that routinized work has been redesigned to increase its interest and appeal to workers, whilst also deriving productive benefits for the organization. Job enrichment and empowerment have been prominent here.

Job enrichment emerged in the late 1960s as a way of providing employees with greater involvement in scheduling and performing their work, engaging their 'higher order' needs—for social contact, challenge, and a sense of completion. The approach derived from the teachings of humanist psychologists, such as Abraham Maslow (earlier discussed). One widely published application was Volvo cars in Sweden. They replaced the traditional assembly line with a sequence of work teams. Each team was given responsibility for deciding its preferred ways of operating—as long as they delivered the required output and quality. In effect, the new system formally harnessed some of the informal peer-management methods discovered by the Western Electric researchers in the 1930s, but now part of a culture of greater trust. Today, an enriched computer-assembly process, for example, would shift a worker who solders a single component again and again, into a team around a workstation that assembles the whole computer, while enjoying social interaction and chat. Team members would be able to share and rotate different tasks and organize their own breaks, and they would all have a stake in the completed product.

Recently, the principles of job enrichment have been merged with workplace empowerment to create 'self-managed work teams' and 'high performance work systems'. The empowerment dimension means that employees can take on some of the discretion and responsibility once held by their supervisors or bosses: they no longer have to refer upwards for permission or checking on particular issues or decisions. Trust is reconfigured in this arrangement, a potentially better foundation for self-development and a sense of achievement at work. In principle, empowerment can do much to humanize the workplace—if it is not undermined by other agendas. For example, having stripped out layers of supervision to save costs, empowerment can appear as an excuse by management to intensify work, pushing more work and responsibility onto relatively fewer people, often for no extra reward. When empowerment is imposed by an employer suspicions are, understandably, aroused: forced empowerment feels like—and is—a contradiction in terms.

Empowerment and enrichment represent a tilt in the balance of power away from unilateral management control. But there are some bold industrial leaders who have gone much further. Ricardo Semler, majority owner of the Brazilian Semco Group, is one. This is how the company describes itself:

> A company full of crazy people? A Group of nutters? If you think that Semco is something along these lines, you're not entirely wrong. However, it is not by chance that unconventional ideas are created at this company. They are created and managed within an open management model, different from conventional models and this is exactly what we want.

Since the mid-1980s, Semler's 'open' approach to management has created a world-leading manufacturer of industrial equipment and high tech software, employing over 3,000 people worldwide. Semler's personal philosophy is fundamentally humanistic. He believes that the traditional preoccupation with control wears down the human potential on which the organization depends. A satisfying, worthwhile work life, he asserts, is achieved through the minimum of control and the fewest structural barriers.

The implications for his company have been far reaching. People set their own working hours and salaries. Everybody shares in the profits and receives regular reports on how well the company is trading. Employees can close a factory or veto a deal on a show of hands. The CEO designation circulates regularly between a group of executives, and everyone else has the title of 'associate'. Associates choose and evaluate their own managers, and there are seats at board level for associates. Semler's methods may, of course, not suit all organizations, but they can be credited with injecting new life into the meaning of empowerment and responsibility at work.

Extreme workers and presenteeism

The health risks of long working hours have been well documented: they are likely to cause psychological and physical illnesses. Collective bargaining regularly focuses on working hours, and many countries regulate them. For example, a European Union directive stipulates that people should work no more than forty-eight hours a week. Yet long working hours remain. In South Korea it is not unusual to work an 8 a.m. to 10 p.m. day, and similarly in Japan. In the UK, USA, Canada, and Australia over a quarter of managers and professional workers work more than fifty hours a week, some over eighty hours. Long hours are especially prevalent in mining, retailing, transport, oil and gas exploration, law, and financial trading.

Working long and punishing hours can be culturally pervasive, but for some individuals it is akin to an addiction, described in one US study as 'living the American Dream on steroids'. There are people who freely admit to incessant, self-induced, pressure, characteristics of what has been called a 'Type A' personality: very ambitious, highly competitive, aggressive, and preoccupied with status. Type As are said to be drawn to jobs that have tight deadlines, an unpredictable flow, extensive responsibilities, heavy travel, events outside regular hours, and round-the-clock availability. The financial rewards can be considerable for Type As, but the adrenalin rush is even more satisfying. Typing personality in this simple way has its appeal, especially in popular psychology, but its scientific record is controversial, and sounds a cautionary note on the robustness of the Type A designation. Nevertheless, we know that many extreme workers have strained relationships with their spouses or partners and are frequently absent parents. They can suffer insomnia, drink too much alcohol, not have enough exercise, and rely on medications to relieve anxiety.

Presenteeism

Presenteeism is part of this picture. Presenteeism is the belief that not being seen at work, not being physically at one's desk, will be interpreted as lack of commitment and therefore a risk to one's advancement or livelihood. Presenteeism norms ('I really can't leave before my boss'; 'Not turning up, for whatever reason, is really frowned upon'; 'They think we're superhuman') can tie people to their desks or duties well beyond the 9 to 5, while trapping people who feel ill:

> I can't ring in at ten o'clock and say 'I can't, I feel dreadful tonight.' You just drag yourself along and work. (Night-shift nurse)

> Sometimes, it's like you wouldn't mind if your head rolled off your body. You feel clogged up and hazy. The pressure makes you want to close your eyes. It's hard to focus. You end up just muddling through. (Design engineer and migraine sufferer)

When an employer rewards people for coming in and staying late then, save serious illness, that is what people are likely to do. And where there is a norm that illness is perceived as a personal weakness or poor commitment, then people are apt to drag themselves into work, regardless. While presenteeism norms are perhaps understandable for some hard-pressed organizations, they do contain destructive potential—on the well-being of workers and on the very effectiveness of the organization.

Downshifting

> For a long time I had thought about not having to work really, really hard 5/6 days a week in a very stressful

thankless role in retail. Yes...I was paid a fairly good salary in comparison to others, but, you don't realize how much you get wrapped up in this lifestyle, wasting money, wasting precious hours of your life and knocking years off your life through being stressed for someone else's pocket. With this money, you get sucked into consumerism thinking that you need all the trending gadgets and gizmos, twice a year holidays, expensive brand clothes, expensive food, to feel you need to be happy, so easily through the media, peer pressure and social networking.

One day feeling so tired and depressed...I just gave in my notice, to leave my middle management role at work, and with that reduced my working hours to go and work for, and alongside my partner who then had his own business working in a recycle centre. To cut a very long story short, I am now working 25 hours a week, which for a single wage earner is quite low, and in return I am able to do things properly. I work for myself running a market stall in a beautiful part of North Devon. One has to stand and look up at the rainbow, instead of running fast to find the pot of gold. My life is my own now, and I feel I am very rich.

This person is a downshifter. Downshifters can be found across all walks of life, although most have been fairly successful in their previous job or career. What they share is disaffection with a consumerist, job-centred, lifestyle: 'the trouble with the rat race is, even if you win, you are still a rat'. Material wealth, as many studies show, offers no guarantee of contentment. Happiness does not increase proportionally to the size of the wage packet. Downshifters have sought a simpler way, some by exchanging city homes for countryside living. Many opt for work that is intrinsically satisfying, and a way of life that gives them more time for friends and family. Downshifters rarely go for extreme self-denial. They typically aim for a comfortable life, but less harried and hurried, and no longer dominated by a wearisome or unfulfilling job.

Downshifting can be seen as a twenty-first-century post-materialist phenomenon. It is a radical response to the emptiness that some people feel as they chase ever more goods and services—the conventional icons of success in materialistic economies. Across Europe, there are an estimated 12 million downshifters and rising; 3.7 million are in the UK. In the USA and Australia, over 8 per cent of the working population have downshifted. Most downshifters report satisfaction, if not delight, with their move. But—and not without irony—sustaining a downshifted lifestyle favours those who have wealth-cushioning to fall back upon. Even allowing for their now less-profligate ways, some downshifters with young families have found the reduction in income difficult to adjust to.

A positive solution?

Opting out of mainstream work is a personal solution to an unfulfilling job or career, but it is not a social solution to unfulfilling jobs. Recently, the positive movement in social science has attempted to grasp this tough nettle. Taking over from where job enrichment and empowerment left off, and rooted in American positive psychology, the positive movement urges a reorganization of work to liberate feelings of positiveness and happiness-inducing experiences. It coincides with disenchantment with gross domestic product as an index of societal well-being. Some suggest that we would do better to turn to a measure of 'gross national happiness' to capture a truer, person-centred, picture of the health and wealth of a nation.

Positive theorists and practitioners have focused on various aspects of work—its values, its leadership, its content, and its methods. They argue that selfishness, greed, and winning at all costs have undermined, and often displaced, the capacity for altruism and mutual tolerance. Optimism and positive thinking are squeezed out when fault, blame, and fear pervade an organization. The merits of 'authentic' leadership are stressed—leaders who are ethically sound, confident, and resilient. An asset-based approach to management, such as Appreciative Inquiry, is preferable to a deficit one. Appreciative Inquiry turns traditional deficiency thinking on its head. It seeks to build on the positive by emphasizing people's personal resources and strengths, not their weaknesses. Instead of asking 'What's wrong with you?' or 'What should be fixed?' it asks 'What's working well for you?' and 'What feels good to you in your work?'

Feeling of flow, argue positive writers, should not be confined to an exclusive minority of workers. Flow is being totally immersed in what you do, fully engaged and 'lost' in your work. Time is not noticed when in flow. Flow is often reported by artists, sculptors, musicians, and athletes, but flow is also achievable in other kinds of work, especially where goals are focused, tasks stretch abilities, and feedback is fast. Managers, for example, are more likely to report feelings of flow when they are involved in non-routine activities, such as planning, problem solving, and evaluations.

The ambitions of the positive movement are laudable—but are they realistic? Competition, self-interest, and aggression are ideologically entrenched, frequently celebrated, values of corporate capitalism. It is a system (sometimes called the 'least worse' of the world's economic ideologies) that certainly has its downsides, and here positive interventions may well help to smooth the rougher edges. Yet creating affirmative experiences at work is hemmed in by the economic culture. Many routine deskilled and unskilled jobs are now irreversibly built into our economy to provide the mass of products and services that we take for granted, and are not especially conducive to deep worker-engagement. The supermarket checkout clerk, suggest some positive promoters, would do well to pay genuine attention to customers and benefit from the feeling of well-being and flow that this brings. Possibly; but supermarket checkouts are designed for fast, fleeting interactions. In busy and congested times, they can be hassle for all, especially for low-paid checkout staff who are measured on the flow of customers, not their feelings of flow. There has to be something personally meaningful in the content or context of work to feel bright about.

Where jobs have the potential for flow experiences, then liberating that flow from cumbersome or oppressive controls can indeed be a positive step. Beyond this, positive organizational initiatives may help relieve some of the tedium and stresses of work, making it a less unhappy experience—but not necessarily a happy one. And happiness itself is curious phenomenon. We learn what happiness feels like from our unhappy moments, and what is positive or happy to one person can be ambiguous, even negative, to another. Happiness is more likely to be a transient than continuous experience, which makes it problematic to simply 'fix', capture, or prearrange. A Pollyanna perspective on work—'always look on the bright side'—is rarely in tune with the uneven mix of emotions that real-time daily work generates.

Chapter 6
Emotion at work

It should not seem strange that work involves emotions. Yet, until relatively recently, academic portrayals of work life were reticent about emotion. Emotion was often sanitized in terms such as attitudes, preferences, and satisfactions. Strong emotions, especially, were seen to impede the smooth running of the rational enterprise, like sand in the organization's machinery. In the late 1940s, social theorist Max Weber noted that it was the very absence of emotion that sustained the 'ideal' bureaucracy. Bureaucracy develops, Weber wrote, 'the more perfectly...the more it is "dehumanized", the more completely it succeeds in eliminating from official business love, hatred, and all purely personal, irrational, and emotional elements which escape calculation'.

Weber's portrayal of an emotion-free bureaucracy summons up images of bureaucrats located in the offices (*bureaux*) of public and private organizations, impersonally and dispassionately applying administrative rules. Rarely can a complex organization be sustained without some bureaucratic control, which, at best, ensures fairness, consistency, and impartiality. However, it is its worst features that are remembered most, where set procedures and rules become ends in themselves. They are ingrained in totalitarian organizations and states, where obsessive bureaucracy stifles creative energy, discretion, and individuality, suppressing the very passions that human beings live and work by. A flourishing organization works with, not against, emotion.

Emotions can be seen as an indelible feature of working life, the prime medium through which we act and relate to one another, shaping and lubricating an organizational order. Feelings such as pride, joy, happiness, trust, love, and excitement, as well as fear, shame, anxiety, guilt, anger, and sorrow, are fundamental to what we do. They are implicated in how hard or reluctantly we work, how close or distant we are from our colleagues or bosses, and how committed or indifferent we are to our jobs.

An emotionful work life does not mean an emotion free-for-all. Emotion *work* permeates daily experiences. It is the constant interplay or tension between what we subjectively feel and what we can show or express—to whom, when, and where. Culture—societal and organizational—plays a pivotal role here. It frames how we should act and defines the currency of the socioemotional economy: the emotions we exchange to sustain or reset social bonds—a hand on the shoulder, a note of praise or compassion, a disapproving glance, a statement of appreciation, a hug or embrace. How masculinized or feminized is the setting? How interpersonal or impersonal is the work? How hierarchical or egalitarian is it?

Different physical zones of the workplace add materially to the emotion mosaic. The committee rooms, the corridors, the water cooler, the washrooms are, through quiet social consensus, invisibly coded to permit different degrees of frankness, disclosure, confession, or venting. Managing emotion is a fine-tuned human skill where context matters. A theatre company, engineering factory, hospital, army regiment, or police academy have contrasting emotion norms to which new members are socialized, and which, over time, are tested. Until recently, homosexuality in the American armed forces was handled on a 'don't ask don't tell' principle, allowing gay men and women to serve in the military only if they kept their sexual orientation secret. The emotion work for these recruits could be onerous. They were haunted by the threat of exposure and of possible dismissal from the service.

The springs of emotion

Emotions are richly theorized, a disparate field that can be condensed roughly into three complementary perspectives: psychoanalytic, evolutionary, and social constructionist. Psychoanalysis, as articulated by Sigmund Freud and his followers, focuses primarily on the impact of early-life experiences and unresolved difficulties that are carried into adulthood and the workplace, mostly as unconscious desires and anxieties. Through a psychoanalytic lens we are all prisoners of our past. Present feelings will often be manifestations of past incidents, difficulties, fears, or traumas, and unless they are openly (and often lengthily) examined, old emotional sores can continue to fester. It follows that, beneath a semblance of order in work organizations is a cauldron of concealed agendas, suppressed or repressed anxieties, and unfulfilled desires, pushing and pulling people in directions that are often beyond their conscious control. Irrationality, therefore, is endemic to the human actor and human organization.

Evolutionary psychologists think rather differently about emotion. They posit a clutch of human signature-emotions—particularly anger, jealousy, regret, disgust, and love—that have been central to the survival of our species. Caring for kin, finding shelter and food, avoiding predators, and attracting mates required different biological programmes to be successful, and emotions evolved appropriately. In the workplace, these emotional impulses are still with us, stirred during competition for scarce resources, in office romances and other personal attachments, in protecting status, in the scramble for promotion and recognition, and in privileging male aggression and dominance.

The third perspective is held by social constructionists. They argue that our individual and ancient pasts tell only part of the emotion story, and the lesser part at that. Societal culture holds the trump card, to play a major role in what we subjectively feel and what we can emotionally express, and the two do not always correspond. We feel low but have to appear cheerful to our workmates; we show disappointment at a colleague's poor sales results, although privately feel rather pleased and a bit smug. But 'private' feelings, from this point of view, are not always as idiosyncratic or private as we might believe. They, too, can be overwritten by social conventions and norms on what we *should* be subjectively feeling, such as sadness at a funeral, joy at a new birth in the family, or love towards a partner. Social learning provides a delicate decorum around which our personal feelings and displayed emotions are arranged—an exquisite, though far from foolproof, achievement of civilized life (we can 'get it wrong', misinterpreting or misattributing another's emotion signals). There are unwritten emotion rules, roles, and scripts to internalize if we are to become mature social actors, making emotions part social performance and part personal readout on how well we are relating and doing.

Decisions, decisions

The nuanced view of emotion has challenged traditional conceptions about thinking and feeling. Thinking and feeling, or cognition and emotion, have long been regarded as essentially distinct processes. Rather like the strictures that judges place on juries to 'not let your emotions sway your deliberations', we are able to suspend our feelings when we make our analyses and judgements—or so it appears. Recent research has cast doubt on this. Various studies suggest that, as we go about our daily endeavours and decision-making, our feelings and thinking interpenetrate in complex ways, often beyond our conscious control. Put simply, they indicate that, without our emotions, our cognitive processes would often grind to a halt—we would get stuck, unable sensibly to sort our priorities, reach conclusions, or actually make decisions.

When we examine what organizational decision-makers actually do, they repeatedly fail the textbook-rationality test. The rational decision-maker is advised to list and prioritize their goals, lay out alternative ways of achieving each of them, calculate the different likelihoods of success, and finally adopt the avenue that will deliver maximum return. That is what it takes to be rational. There is mounting evidence that workplace decisions, especially complex ones, are rarely, if ever, made in such a computational way. They are typically tackled messily and intuitively, with and through emotion. At best we 'satisfice', muddle through, to reach a 'good enough' solution. As one manager confesses: 'I have to sort through so many issues at once…I use defence mechanisms to deal with the overload…This is an uncomfortable process for me.…I create smoke or offer some grand theory as the only ways to keep my sanity…One of the frustrations is that I don't want to tell my people that their number one problems have lower priorities than they think they should get.'

Decisions often implicate different stakeholders, the outcomes potentially contentious and readily politicized. In sometimes heated exchanges, people bargain, persuade, rant, clash, sulk, excite, despair, become angry, frustrated…. a socioemotional melting pot that is remote for the axioms of rationality. Yet appearing rational—'not emotional'—is accorded high cultural value. Workplace decisions are readily reconstructed and presented in rational narrative, ensuring that the chimera of rationality lives on.

Emotional labour

There are occupations that require particular emotions of their members, such as seriousness, enthusiasm, joy, passion, or zeal. In this manner, routine emotion work is transformed into *emotional labour*; emotions are an explicit or implicit part of the employment contract. Emotional labour is especially evident in the service industry where once-idiosyncratic features of the sales demeanour have been lifted, sifted, and corporatized. As this sector has become more homogenized, the 'smile that sells', especially, has been recast as an emotional competency to be trained and monitored by the employer. Public and private services that were once culturally distinctive for their spontaneity, indifference, or grunts have given way to scripted, North American style, ebullience. It can be encountered across the globe in hotels, rail and bus services, banks, supermarkets, airlines, fast-food outlets, call centres, and themed entertainments. A fly-on-the-wall TV documentary contained the following scene from inside a McDonald's restaurant in the UK. An especially keen assistant manager bounces up to Sal in her short break from flipping burgers:

MANAGER. Morning Sal! How you feeling today?

SAL. Fine.

MANAGER. Now look, when I say how you feeling, I want you to say 'outstanding!'

SAL. OK. [She looks bewildered]

MANAGER. So how you feeling today!?

SAL. Outstanding.

MANAGER. OK. *Really* get motivation. I'm telling all the crew today, when I ask them how they feel I want them to say 'outstanding!' Go like that with your arms [he thrown his arms outwards].

SAL. OK.

MANAGER. So how you feeling today!?

SAL. Outstanding! [She mimics him with obvious feigned enthusiasm]

Here the employer is specifying not just the technical skills needed to perform the job, but the emotional ones too. There are company emotion rules, some posted behind the checkout till ('Smile!'). Training sessions and detailed manuals are part of the package of controls. Disney theme park 'cast' are instructed to 'always make eye contact and smile; greet and welcome each and every guest; say "thank you" to each and every guest; demonstrate patience and honesty in handling complaints'. In insurance training there are exhortations to sales trainees to 'fake it 'til you make it' if they have difficulty producing the required demeanour, while call-line operators are instructed to 'smile down the phone'.

Formalized dress and body codes augment the approved performance. They range from the titillating to the conservative and traditional, such as Disney's precise instructions on hair length and fingernail length ('to not exceed one-forth of an inch beyond the fingertip'). Here, emotional labour merges with aesthetic labour: workers are expected to embody the visual image of the brand. Deviations are not tolerated—as Harrods' assistant Melanie Stark was to discover in 2011. She was a person who never wore make-up, which soon brought her into conflict with Harrods' 'face code'. It stipulated: 'full makeup at all time: base, blusher, full eyes (not too heavy), lipstick, lip liner and gloss are worn at all time and maintained discreetly (please take into account the store display lighting which has a "washing out" effect).' In no uncertain terms, she was informed by her manager that she had two options: to wear make-up or leave. She left: 'I was appalled. It was insulting. Basically, it was implying it would be an improvement. I don't understand how they think it is OK to say that.... I just could not see how, in this day and age, Harrods could take away my right to choose whether to wear it or not.'

For corporately scripted service workers, emotional labour can be a mixed experience. Some quite enjoy it. They see it as a game, an exchange of superficial pleasantries where the fun is in pulling off a good performance, but to be switched off soon after the event. Others are not so accepting. For them it can be a relentless, stressful, pretence: putting on a smile, regardless of what is privately felt:

> When you wake up in the morning, turn on your smile on. Don't turn it back off again until you go to sleep.

Some days I just can't do it. There's only so much you can smile and put on a phoney face. Sometimes I'm actually too tired or bored or pissed off at the world to pretend I am happy, but my jobs require that I am happy all the time.

In low-status, low-pay service work, there may be little to smile about, but not to smile can be unforgivable. Some employers install 'smile police' to pose as customers, while others rely on spy cameras, the monitoring of phone calls, or customer satisfaction questionnaires. Still others go for a blunt, confrontational, approach: 'I'll go up in their faces and I go, "What is wrong?"' says a Brooklyn Burger King manager. 'They look at me like they don't know what I am doing. "What is wrong with your face?" I am smiling. You don't know what it is like?' (See Figure 11.)

Coping with emotional labour over time can be a testing experience. A surface mask can crack under sustained pressure, something that sociologist Arlie Hochschild observed in her landmark study of flight attendants:

> A young businessman said to a flight attendant, 'Why aren't you smiling?' She put her tray back on the food cart and said, 'I'll tell you what. You smile first, then I'll smile.' The businessman smiled at her. 'Good,' she replied. 'Now freeze and hold that for fifteen hours.'

Workers of this sort may seek relief in a backstage zone, such as the galley area of an aircraft, the restaurant lobby, or staff rest-room. They are places where different emotion rules apply, a temporary amnesty from their usual emotional labours. There, the 'obnoxious' passenger, client, or customer can safely be derided, in the presence of a receptive audience of peers.

Some companies are keen to attract employees who are prepared to 'really take on board' and internalize the company's message and training; to 'really feel' for the customer. The service worker is encouraged to fuse their personality with their work role; to

11. Putting on the smile that sells

synchronize their feelings with the required corporate line. Those susceptible to such injunctions are well-inducted emotional labourers and less fazed by pressures or inconsistencies experienced by their surface-acting counterparts. But outside of work they can find it difficult to extract themselves from the roles in which they have become so engrossed.

Not just service workers

There are doctors, dentists, nurses, counsellors, social workers, teachers, managers, lawyers, police, journalists, and other people-facing professionals for whom emotional labour is implicit to their professionalism. It is learned on the job and key to how they relate to their clients or customers. To do it well enhances their rapport and care. To do it poorly can compromise their professional credibility and standing. Implicit emotion rules include: appearing serious and attentive, not being over familiar, not ignoring a client's feelings, not being patronizing, not appearing sexist, not expressing irritation, and so forth. The emotional labour can be demanding, especially when they face 'awkward' or 'challenging' people—as the following male nurse tells:

> I work in a crazy, busy, emergency department with a lot of, well let's be honest, scum and addicts come in for free shelter, food, drugs, etc. I seem to get the patients who are rude and constantly degrade me. I had one such charmer last night. Every other sentence out of his mouth was, 'Why are you a nurse? I want a female nurse. I don't want no *** touching me.... You're too stupid to be a doctor, I don't want your hands on me.' I know I should realize what is going on and just let it slide off, but sometimes I get so angry. It made me wanna give him a less-than-gentle catheter. How can I deal with offensive patients like this?

Can emotions be intelligent?

Educationalists and psychologists have long recognized that IQ, or cognitive intelligence, is not the only kind of intelligence we possess. There are others, such as musical intelligence and bodily kinaesthetic intelligence. But it was not until the 1990s that the notion of emotional intelligence (EI) came to the fore, in fair measure due to promotional efforts of science journalist Daniel Goleman. In his provocatively titled book *Emotional Intelligence: Why it Can Matter More Than IQ* he argued that much is missed if we place abstract thinking, memory, and verbal reasoning, the contents of traditional intelligence tests and mainstream education, on an exclusive pedestal. Dealing with emotional information is just as important; often more so. It is central to the content and outcome of life's social interactions and transactions, and is especially relevant to effective leadership. All these require proficiency at recognizing and interpreting emotions in oneself and others, and then deploying them wisely; in other words, emotional intelligence.

In the popular press, emotional intelligence has been widely canvassed as a major discovery, a 'magic bullet' for success. One national newspaper has dubbed it 'the final frontier in the quest for organizational excellence'. It has created opportunities for business consultants to evaluate and raise your EI. Some are extravagant in their claims ('55 Ways to Improve your Emotional Intelligence'), guaranteeing the positive changes that will ensue.

The facts and fashionability of EI are easily muddled, and magic bullets do have the habit of not delivering their magic. When we unpack the research evidence on emotional intelligence there is a fair amount of confusion. Different authors propose different combinations of competences and attributes to define EI, while not all EI measures (and there are many) produce similar results. For example, on self-report measures, men judge themselves as more emotionally intelligent than their objectively tested EI indicates. For women, the results are precisely the opposite. In other words, men appear to overestimate their emotion skills, while women underestimate theirs. Some researchers claim that emotional intelligence works best at the 'tipping point' of performance, when IQ has reached its limits and done its best. Others, wedded more to the interpenetration of cognition and emotion, assert that emotional intelligence infuses all our interpersonal judgements and decisions—it is constantly and quietly at work in the background.

Can EI be increased, or are you stuck with what you have? This question is complicated by controversy over how EI is created in the first place. Two views predominate. The first is that EI is formed in childhood, to mature by the time adulthood is reached—and it is gender skewed. Girls become more accomplished than boys at recognizing and verbally expressing emotions because they are often exposed, earlier, to a wider range of emotionalities from their parents. Boys, in competitive environments, learn to minimize emotions linked to vulnerability, guilt, fear, and pain, and to avoid expressing weaknesses. Other than superficial shifts, changes of EI in adulthood are unlikely.

The second view is that, with expert teaching, EI can be learned at almost any time in the life. From this perspective, EI is understood as a mix of skills at recognizing and appraising emotions. People can be classroom trained in them, rather like learning a new language. Many EI courses are built on this assumption and some changes have been recorded. But what remains in doubt is the extent and durability of the training effects.

Bullying and harassment

Our negative emotions—envies, anger, prejudices, insecurities, fears, and anxieties—interweave our work experiences. Normally they are self-managed, held beneath the surface. But there are occasions when they are expressed more directly and more forcefully—as bullying and harassment. Bullying and harassment are estimated to affect over 12 million workers across Europe and over a third of the US workforce. One study notes that, in 2006, a fifth of all UK employees said they had experienced some form of bullying in the previous two years. In recent years there has been increasing concern about abusive practices in society, which has heightened awareness of bullying.

A bullied victim can be ridiculed, publicly humiliated, frightened, or physically assaulted. Their emotional injuries include depression, nervousness, insomnia, apathy, and fear of social groups. Bullies typically torment and wear down their victims, undermining their personal or professional integrity. There may be a single bully or a like-minded group who mob their victim. Being part of a mob, or 'group mind', accelerates deindividuation—the dissipation of feelings of personal responsibility or culpability. It fast erodes the moral checks and balances that normally regulate an individual's actions. It is a sobering observation that the most moderate and law-abiding of citizens can 'turn' remarkably when part of a predatory group, be it in the workplace, the football terrace, or an urban riot.

Bullying is nearly always associated with power differences, either explicitly (by superiors) or implicitly within the informal order of the workgroup. The victim's lower status can itself be a sufficient excuse to bully, but so can other apparent differences or distinctions, such as work performance, ethnicity, sexual preference, age, gender, or mental or physical handicap. The arbitrariness says far more about the bully than the victim— although that is not necessarily how it is felt by the victim: 'why me?' Bullies' actions are often rooted in their own troubled life, some having being bullied themselves, their difficulties acted out by diminishing others. Many are unusually narcissistic, preoccupied with drawing attention to themselves, emotionally cold, and incapable of empathizing with their victims. Individual bullies rarely acknowledge that they have bullied, and readily rationalize their actions: the victim 'asked for it', 'is far too touchy', 'is exaggerating', 'is a real loser'.

Bullying can be embedded in an organization's culture or sub-culture, 'not noticed' or ignored by management. When organizations are blind to bullying, predatory behaviour can thrive: 'it's just a normal part of the way we work'; 'it toughens people up', 'we don't see it as bullying', 'it's more of a game and joke'. Such accounts can be found in work settings as varied as firefighters, schools, social services, police academies, the military, banks, and postal work—as the fate of a young British postman reveals. Postman Jermaine Lee took his own life in 1999 (he was found hanged from a belt at his home). We can only guess at the level of anguish that led Lee to his tragic action, but his employer, Royal Mail, mounted the most extensive investigation in its history to uncover a trail of constant bullying by a group of staff at the depot where he worked. The investigators proposed fifty recommendations for change 'to prevent a similar tragedy'.

Bullying tends to be more prevalent in organizations when there is obsession with short-term results, 'making the numbers'; where aggressiveness is regarded as a virtue; where fear is used as a motivator; and where discipline from top management is inconsistent or absent. A number of these conditions were present in a private care home for young people in Bristol, UK, in 2011. The young women and men residents, all with severe learning difficulties, were subjected to a relentless regime of abuse for the 'amusement' of staff. They suffered systematic physical brutality and humiliation by the very people supposed to be caring for them. A senior 'carer' led the tormenting, enthusiastically followed by his subordinate staff. A graphic public exposé by an investigative journalist forced the closure of the home and prosecution of its staff.

Anti-bullying policies are the first line of defence against bullying in the workplace. There is now an armoury of human resource procedures that can assist, including coaching and counselling, education and training. Culturally entrenched bullying is the most difficult to tackle because it traps its victims and stifles its critics. Public exposure—by a regulator, whistleblower, or the media—can be one of the few avenues of redress for victims.

Sexual harassment

Sexual harassment is unwanted, offensive, sexual attention: remarks, innuendo, touching, or intimidation. Like bullying—with which it overlaps—its profile as a social problem has been raised considerably over recent decades. Sexual harassment is infused with gender ideology and passion, and is a major rallying point for feminist scholars, gay and lesbian pressure groups, the media, and law makers.

The sexual harasser and victim can be of any gender, and not necessarily opposite genders. The proportion of men claiming sexual harassment at work (by another man or a woman) has been gradually increasing over the years, but the dominant picture is of women sexually harassed by men. In the USA, for example, women comprised 84 per cent of legal filings for sexual harassment in 2011. Women's predicament is, in part, a consequence of their wider, societal, subordination, coupled with a male view of acceptable sexual conduct. The 'availability' of women, buttressed by gender stereotypes (women as 'soft', 'temperamental'), adds force to the harasser's justifications and power. At its most flagrant, sexual harassment is openly coercive, such as sexual demands by a boss, laced with threats for non-compliance—perhaps job loss or delayed promotion. More diffuse is a male/macho organizational culture that deprecates and marginalizes women. It is where lewd or suggestive remarks, sexual jokes, intimate questions about sex life, and the objectifying of women in sexually explicit images or videos circulate freely. Women who object simply provoke further unwanted attention, while those who keep silent, feeling intimidated, are readily misread as 'not minding' or 'enjoying it':

> All the signs are there but I'm just having trouble believing it's happening to me. I'm getting sexually harassed at work. My boss's crony (whom I don't specifically report to but is in the chain of command) makes me feel uncomfortable on a daily basis, be it by looks, comments, or literally following me down the hall. He even suggests alternatives to my clothes 'to make things look more casual.' I've spoken to him several times and even used the words 'sexual harassment' in my pleas to back off. I've come to an impasse…

Particularly vulnerable are low-status, low-paid service workers. Some hotel cleaning staff, for instance, have to enter the private space of a guest's bedroom, places that have long been associated with sexual flings, adult movies, and prostitution, and where male guests, should they feel inclined, are liberated from their normal sexual constraints. A correspondent in the *Guardian* newspaper dryly captures the scene: 'The life of a hotel maid is not an easy one, with naked men flaunting their wares, verbal abuse, lecherous suggestions and personal hygiene standards that would shame a chimp.' There are accounts of room-cleaning staff retaliating when sexually harassed, only to be disciplined by their employer for their actions. Others can become entangled in wider power dynamics, as was the case of Nafissatou Diallo in 2011.

In much distress, Nafissatou Diallo, a 32-year-old immigrant from Guinea, reported to officials that she had just been raped by a customer in his penthouse suite at a luxury New York hotel where she worked. She had been cleaning his room, presumed unoccupied at the time. Unbeknown to her, the assailant happened to be Dominique Straus-Kahn, then head of the International Monetary Fund—a married Frenchman of considerable wealth and power. In France, he had a reputation for philandering, a fact that many of his compatriots shrugged off as a mild idiosyncrasy of French male behaviour, especially amongst the powerful elite. He was promptly arrested on board a plane about to leave New York, but a district attorney dismissed the case two days later because of 'concerns about the chamber maid's credibility', an allusion to her background and lack of proper residency. The wisdom of the attorney's decision is a matter of dispute, and Nafissatou Diallo responded with a civil suit against her alleged assailant. The case, nevertheless, resonates with others where female victims of sexual harassment or assault appear disadvantaged when pitched against well-resourced, higher-status male defendants, and a male-dominated police and justice system. There is a history of rape cases that tend to favour the alleged perpetrator's version of events, and where female victims feel they are undergoing a further assault in the witness box.

Workplaces are not de-sexualized zones; they are arenas where flirtations, sex gossip, and sexualized humour can flow, and romances come and go. The borders between OK and not OK sexual attention, between the private and the public, are tacitly negotiated and vary between occupations and cultures. There is, inevitably, ambiguity or greyness at the boundaries, such that accusations of sexual harassment can become mired in contested perceptions of intentionality and acquiescence. These issues are intensified in workplaces where women are in the minority, or where their work emphasizes their physical attractiveness or glamour—such as flight attendants, hotel receptionists, bar girls, and pole dancers.

Sexual harassment has sparked intense debates about how women are perceived and treated, and legal measures against sexual harassment in the workplace are now common to many countries. Yet legal instruments, as important as they are, can only scratch the surface of embedded cultural attitudes that objectify women at work.

Chapter 7
Virtual work

'The virtual society' is a fitting description for the way that information technologies have penetrated almost all aspects of our lives. In technologically developed societies most occupations are in some way virtualized. The sensory cues once assumed essential for doing work and building relationships—touch, physical presence, face-to-face exchanges—are much reduced or completely bypassed.

This mediation of social reality has prompted a revision of the traditional notion of 'going to work' because, for a growing number of workers, there is no physical work organization to go to. Their organization exists in cyberspace; a digital wirearchy of electronic connections that have no fixed workstations or offices. Work occurs wherever the worker happens to be. The pace and extent of virtual work has intrigued a broad spectrum of experts, from sociologists and psychologists to urban planners and communication specialists. How can people function meaningfully in such a technologically mediated environment? What are the gains for employers and workers? And what is lost?

Telework

Telework and telecommuting capture a core provision of virtuality—to be able to work at almost any distance (*tele*) from a colleague, customer, work team, or manager. Telework surmounts geographical and time barriers, the humble telephone line morphed into a high-speed internet connection, alongside exceptionally portable smartphones, smart cards, laptops, and tablets. There is the familiar sight of teleworkers with open laptops and buzzing mobile phones in airports and on commuter trains, and evocative images of them on remote beaches, up mountains, and in relaxing cafés. The extreme teleworker can work from anywhere there is a digital signal, although the common locations are home, car, or a customer's place of business. Some teleworkers use touchdown centres and satellite offices to periodically consolidate their work.

Teleworkers can be self-employed or employees. In the USA they make up some 11 per cent of the working population; in the UK, 8 per cent, a doubling since the 1990s. Germany, Sweden, and the Netherlands top the European league of teleworkers, each with over 17 per cent of the workforce. Building an accurate profile of teleworkers is not easy. Available records suggest that they are most likely to be 30–55-year-old males in professional or skilled jobs. Employers tend not to favour career beginners as teleworkers, and women are more likely to be offered clerical tele jobs, usually working from home. The 'digital divide' distorts the picture: there are people who do not have access to personal computers or internet connectivity because of their poverty, geographical location, or lack of relevant skills.

There is every indication that telework will continue to grow as ever faster, cheaper, and more flexible communication technologies are produced, and as the digital divide is bridged. Telework certainly holds the potential to democratize work. It can reach communities in remote rural and deprived urban settings, where workers are not highly mobile and unemployment rates are high. The widespread availability of mobile phones, for instance, has helped low-income groups in the Caribbean region. The phone sustains their micro-businesses and economic engagements, as well as cross-border business trading, social chat, child support, and housekeeping decisions.

For some employers, the attractions of teleworking are considerable. It can reduce or eliminate office costs and increase productivity. Teleworkers are, on average, 20 per cent more productive than their office-based colleagues, in part because of the blurring of work and non-work hours. Telework helps maintain organizational operations during external disruptions, such as severe weather or strikes. It can also attract a wider-than-usual pool of eligible job candidates, appealing to people who live in out-of-the-way places, and to those unable to find work because of their disability or health problems. Telework is commonly credited with being more environmentally friendly, involving fewer vehicle miles and less pollution, and where the daily travel to work is removed or much reduced—a welcome relief to many urban commuters. Indeed, it is the convenience of teleworking that is often emphasized in company recruitment drives:

> This is the frontline of our business. Bright, upbeat, professional people delivering an excellent service to our valued customers…
> [Y]ou'll be working from home, which means no daily commute, no having to go out on bitter winter mornings or worrying about getting home on time. Enjoy all the benefits of working for a large organisation but in the comfort of your own home. (Automobile Association, UK, 2011)

All joy?

Tales from teleworkers vary. Some are euphoric: telework can be a perfect solution for people seeking an improved work–life balance:

> I thoroughly enjoy working from home, especially on those mornings when there is 4 inches of snow on top of 1 inch of ice, I don't have to tackle the roads. I like the fact that after my shift is over, it's over, no travel time, no rush hour, no added stress, and because I work mostly early morning shifts. I find I am less irritable

and much happier since I started this job. I also want to note that, at 27 years old, I was already sick of dealing with the office politics and playground mentality found in most office environments, here in my 'office' there is none of that, well except when my 6 year old is home, but I expect it from her. This is the best decision I ever made.

I started to look for ways to work at home, and keep away from office politics and corporate wheels, to help me stay 'in charge' of my life. I wanted to decide who, when, where and how I should work. My health depended on it. My inner spirit always wanted to be 'her own boss'. Well, I started to notice and took action. That was when I started with a people friendly company and I will never feel the same again. Telework is my life…I wouldn't give it up for any gold in the world.

Yet there is a flipside. Some teleworkers become jaded as the early advantages and pleasures fade. The immediate presence of work, at any time of the day, can create stress and tension at home. Teleworking is also, by its very nature, isolating: the daily corridor conversations and social life of the workplace are no more. The less self-reliant are vulnerable in these circumstances: they feel alone, marooned with their technology. Career-minded teleworkers speak about their fears of being 'out of the loop', invisible when decisions are being made about promotion and advancement.

Not all employers warm to telework. Some worry about a loss of control over employees who are not physically present: can they be trusted? There are employers who, in the first instance, prefer to dip their toes in the water, granting telework to just some of their staff. However, a danger is that this is perceived by the others as unfair, creating resentment and division. Telework, it seems, is not a practice that an employer can simply bolt on to existing workplace ways. It requires close attention to how it can affect the organization's culture, coherence, and management methods, especially the extent of trust between employer and employee. Fifty years ago, work psychologists coined the phrase 'sociotechnical system' to describe the meshing of the social and technological features of an organization. The principle holds for today's telework.

Virtual teams

Face-to-face teams have long been a feature of workplace organization. They can be permanent or temporary, within a function or cross-functional. As organizations have become more fluid and flexible they are often constructed around team-based projects. These have the virtue of bringing together necessary expertise, as and when necessary. A well-run team capitalizes on the skills and strengths of its different members to achieve a synergistic effect, a resourceful meeting of minds. But this is rarely accomplished without the help of a skilled team leader, someone who anticipates and manages any destructive conflict, and counters groupthink—where dissenters are reluctant to speak out, or defer to the more vocal members. In comparison, how do virtual teams fare?

In the virtual world, there are teams that are exclusively electronic, with no expectation of face-to-face contact. Team members and leaders are acquainted solely thought their virtual presence—emails, text messages, voice recordings, phone calls, webcam images. More common, though, is a mixed modality: team members work virtually for much of the time, but with periodic face-to-face meetings. Members of virtual teams can be physically on the same worksite, even on the same floor of a shared building. But the operational advantages are most apparent when members are separated by considerable distances, even different countries. The Reiter organization, for example, is a Swiss company that provides machinery to yarn producers. When its market switched to China and India it shifted its manufacturing base to those countries, while retaining its research and development facilities in Switzerland, Germany, and the Czech Republic. The separation of core activities created virtual teams that needed to work together and communicate across time and language zones—which they did, with the help of specialized software that could work in five different languages.

Communication curiosities

Compared to co-located, off-line, teams, the quality of communication in virtual teams is generally different, and generally inferior. Text-based communication, particularly, lacks the usual cues, intonations, and facial expressions that inform mutual understandings. It misses or flattens the emotional connections through which relationships are formed and trust is developed, two crucial ingredients of synergistic teamwork. As one virtual team worker member reflected: 'Everything needs to be made more explicit when working virtually than when working face-to-face. Who will do what by when can be confusing in normal teams, but when decided online, without facial and physical responses, role requirements can really get messy.' Virtual teams do generally worse than face-to-face teams when there are tight time constraints, but the difference is less when they have had prior experience working together, with some face-to-face contact.

Sharing a native culture and language helps. Cross-cultural arrangements can be tricky, especially when interpreting colloquialisms, idioms, humour, and irony, shades of meaning rarely captured by language-translation software. Cultural communication norms also vary, such as the appropriateness of self-disclosure, whether disagreements should be expressed, and the meaning of unexplained silence. In a medium that encourages prompt exchanges, silence can be unsettling to team members. Yet, in South Korea, a delayed email response is often taken as a sign of respect, and the Japanese can use silence as a way of preserving harmony.

When quizzed about their failures and successes, virtual team members say that human factors make the difference, not technology. Top of their concerns is the quality of trust and team leadership. On networked projects, particularly, virtual teams often form and disband rapidly, so trust has to be achieved rapidly. The style and content of initial messages—friendly and supportive, or curt and abrupt—can make a major difference. They often fix the quality of perceived trust in the team throughout its short lifespan. Rarely are virtual teams as cohesive as face-to-face ones, so peer groupthink is not so intrusive: members usually feel free to express their queries or dissent to one another. However, hierarchical groupthink can be an issue, such as when a team leader presses hard for a particular outcome.

The virtual team leader's role is different from that of traditional teams. It is focused more on maintaining the logistics of task completion, allocating roles, and attempting to humanize the process—reinforcing the importance of team members as people, not simply virtual resources. Capturing and responding to the mood of the team is a key part of this, which can be challenging when communications are asynchronous, and when even the basics of opening and closing meetings can be awkward, given communication delays.

Cyber incivility, cyber bullying

There is a dark side to virtual work—cyber incivility and cyber bullying. These acts are often associated with adolescents' electronic messaging, where persistent attacks can erode a victim's self-confidence and sometimes trigger self-harm, even suicide. The workplace equivalent is a story less often told:

> I have been cyberbullied by my former program manager for the past 5 years. In 2009, I was forced to resign or be fired. At the time, I was going through some major difficulties. Although I was a very strong and assertive individual, this individual took advantage of my situation in the most humiliating way. Before I chose to resign, I found another job and had to sign an indemnity agreement.
>
> Ten months later, this program manager continued to target me through emails because I was still in the same field but not in

his corporation. I tried to get this behavior to stop but I was not successful. I had no other choice but to take this to a lawyer and took action against all parties that were involved. The unfortunate thing was that it emotionally and financially took a huge toll on me and I had no choice but to drop the case.

Six months after dropping the case, this same program manager emailed me again and started bullying me with the same intimidating comments. This made me feel sick.... This ordeal has left me feeling bad. I am on medication as a result of this whole ordeal and just returned back to work after being off for 8 weeks. This ordeal was a very big part of my life and consumed me for years. I don't know what to do, but I do know that I can't continue to work if this supervisor's unhealthy need to control and over-power me continues.

This person turned eventually to a clinical psychologist for help (whose website features the story). The account contains three important ingredients. The first, like most workplace bullying, is hierarchical power—the boss over the subordinate. The second is the distancing and disinhibiting effect of the virtual medium: the bully can continue to torment without having actually to face their victim, in this case well beyond the formal termination of the work relationship. Finally, there is the bully's enhanced immunity when avenues of recourse for the victim are limited or prohibitively expensive.

Surveys reveal up to one in sixteen people bullied by email or text messages at work, intensified by portable communications outside usual working hours. A study of Australian manufacturing employees found one in ten workers cyberbullied within the previous six months, some on a weekly basis. Typical experiences included being ordered to do work below their level of competence, having allegations made against them, and having information withheld that could directly affect their performance. Some suffered a two-pronged attack—cyber and face to face.

There are some sectors more prone to cyber incivility and cyber bullying than others. They are mostly larger institutions, such as public administration, education, social work, health, transport, and communications. One unusual example is school teaching. Unusual because it shows how virtual technology can sometimes override or reverse the usual formal-power differences that separate bully from victim, harasser from harassed. In this case, it is pupils harassing teachers. Many schoolteachers become accustomed to being the target of spiteful gossip in playgrounds and corridors, but being mocked, threatened, or 'outed' in cyberspace—including silent phone calls, insulting text messages, and emails—has raised the game. Social network sites have enabled pupils, under the cloak of anonymity, to circulate messages to harass or defame their teachers. Surveys of teachers reveal a growing incidence of racist abuse, even death threats, as well as accusations of paedophilia or rape. They come mostly from 11–16-year-olds, but occasionally from pupils as young as 5.

RateMyTeachers.com is designed as 'an educational resource', and ostensibly filters malicious remarks. Founded in America, it is now present in Canada, Ireland, Australia, and the UK. The content filtering, though, is unreliable, with entries such as 'A useless piece of garbage who wouldn't know chemistry if it ran over him'; 'I didn't like her as a teacher...she had a weird smell of vodka to her.' Teachers say such remarks leave them feeling depressed and helpless, robbed of their dignity and self-esteem: 'Well, if that's what they think of me I might as well give up teaching now.'

E-eruptions

Emails have come to dominate much workplace communication, a business tool that has evolved its own conventions. Experienced users often attempt to minimize ambiguity by careful phrasing, sometimes augmented by emoticons. Common courtesies include prompt replies, the spare use of capital letters (signify shouting), and the use of first names to ease familiarity. But in the hurried world of emailing, message meanings can rapidly spiral out of control. Emails are sparse and clunky compared to face-to-face exchanges. Ambiguities are easily magnified and differences inflated. Ensuing frustrations can spark irritation and ignite bouts of flaming: insults and abuse.

A high-profile example occurred in 2005 between two legal secretaries in a prestigious, Australian, law firm. To their embarrassment and ultimate demise, the precise content and outcomes were widely reported in the national press on internet blogs. It all started innocently, about a missing ham sandwich:

KATRINA: Yesterday I put my lunch in the fridge on Level 19 which included a packet of ham, some cheese slices and two slices of bread which was going to be for my lunch today. Overnight it has gone missing and as I have no spare money to buy another lunch today, I would appreciate being reimbursed for it.

MELINDA: There are items fitting your exact description in the level 20 fridge. Are you sure you didn't place your lunch in the wrong fridge yesterday?

KATRINA: Melinda, probably best you don't reply to all next time, would be annoyed (*sic*) to the lawyers. The kitchen was not doing dinner last night, so obviously someone has helped themselves to my lunch. Really sweet of you to investigate for me!

MELINDA: Since I used to be a float and am still on the level 19 email list I couldn't help but receive your ridiculous email—lucky me! You use our kitchen all the time for some unknown reason and I saw the items you mentioned in the fridge so naturally thought you may have placed them in the wrong fridge. Thanks I know I'm sweet and I only had your best interests at heart. Now as you would say, 'BYE'!

KATRINA: I'm not blonde!!!

MELINDA: Being a brunette doesn't mean you're smart though!

KATRINA: I definitely wouldn't trade places with you for 'the world'!

MELINDA: I wouldn't trade places with you for the world... I don't want your figure!

KATRINA: Let's not get person (*sic*) 'Miss Can't Keep A Boyfriend'. I am in a happy relationship, have a beautiful apartment, brand new car, high pay job... say no more!!

MELINDA: Oh my God I'm laughing! happy relationship (you have been with so many guys), beautiful apartment (so what), brand new car (me too), high pay job (I earn more).... say plenty more.... I have five guys at the moment! haha.

The collapse of civility was completed in precisely 44 minutes, as misphrasing and 'advice' fuelled the bad temper. The spat was picked up and forwarded to others in the firm who, in turn, copied it to rival firms. Thereafter it went viral. The main protagonists were treated harshly (some say far too harshly, an over-reaction)— fired for using their work email as a personal messaging system, and for their 'inappropriate' behaviour. The forwarders of the messages were disciplined.

This case reveals that emails can leave a virtual trail for the unwary. The private can become public, embarrassing for the message senders, but also problematic for an employer that is sensitive about its public image. Given this, some employers have chosen to monitor and control what employees do online. Others, perhaps more wisely, have preferred a policy based on education and trust rather than surveillance. A culture of collaboration can often reap longer-term organizational benefits than one built on scrutiny and control.

Tweeting while you work

Web access in the workplace is a gateway to much that is unlikely to be included in an employee's job description. Online shopping, local and national news, live-feeds on sport, personal banking, games, sex sites, YouTube, Facebook, and Twitter—they all actively engage many millions of daily web-users at work. Personal internet usage of this sort divides industry observers, often along morally toned lines. One view is that people who use the web for reasons other than work are shirking their responsibilities. They are 'cyber slackers', 'loafers', or 'slouchers', stealing productive time from their employers. There are prominent cases that bolster this outlook, such as the revelation in 2010 that over two dozen employees of the US Securities and Exchange Commission regularly viewed pornography on their government computers, instead of overseeing the nation's distressed financial system. In response to such events, site-blocking software has been installed by some employers. Facebook is one of the most commonly blocked sites, closely followed by MySpace and YouTube.

But there is a contrasting viewpoint. It acknowledges that the web now permeates all spheres of life, conflating work, leisure, and consumption in unprecedented ways. Many people are now web savvy and move comfortably between different forms of electronic communication, in and out of work. The blurring of communication channels and domains means that personal web usage often provides helpful interludes or breaks in daily work, and does not necessarily compromise overall work performance. For some it is an effective release from stress and can help enhance their performance—a sentiment captured by one web user:

> I'm of the opinion if someone needs internet filtering to be productive you're likely still not going to get the same productivity that you'd get from someone who doesn't need internet filtering.... I enjoy the occasional 5 minute break to clear my thoughts and watch a silly YouTube video, before I start on the next task at hand. I might even share it with my boss, if he's in need of the same thoughts to clear. And guess what? We get shit done. We know what's at stake, and we take our work seriously.

From this point of view, slacking or loafing is a misreading of intention in all but extreme cases. It also suggests that web blocking can be self-defeating for the organization, undermining trust and simply presenting an extra challenge to the committed circumventer (who, anyway, can now surf the web on their smartphone).

Particular social network sites, such as Twitter, often feature in this debate. Tweeting on Twitter is a close substitute for chitchat in the face-to-face world. It is sharing snippets of personal information, ephemeral thoughts, daily musings, and observations. Yet its apparent trivialness disguises one of its virtual virtues: helping to build work relationships in an emotionally anorexic, digital, world. Tweeting goes some way towards creating an intimate personal presence. Indeed, workplace Tweeters often describe how they like to 'take the pulse' on what others are doing, check on their mood, their music, share work gossip, and voice their opinion on current matters—'those little things that go a long way to allow me to maintain some form of relationship'.

In sum, microblogging has become a firm fixture of social networking. Social network sites can, of course, be misused, and there are wary employers who have installed firewalled social network software, such as Yammer, to protect sensitive company information. But others have accepted that microblogging is part-and-parcel of today's socializing, in and beyond work, and have resisted such controls. Microblogs can be seen to play a positive role in supporting virtual work, in relieving the tedium of inherently dull jobs, and in adding new layers of meaning and humanity to workplace relationships.

Chapter 8
Changes and transitions

There has been a hollowing-out of the workforce in the West, a polarization of 'lousy and lovely' jobs. Well-paid managerial jobs have expanded, middle-paid skilled jobs have shrunk, and low-paid service jobs with poor security have increased. This last group includes personal service workers, mostly female housekeepers, hairdressers, child minders, and care assistants. It also contains janitors, cleaners, security officers, and construction labourers, positions that require little formal education and are difficult or expensive to mechanize.

When there is fierce competition for jobs there is a downward drift, a reversal in social mobility as displaced middle-tier workers jockey for the remaining low-wage jobs. Optimists argue that this is a temporary condition: it will take some while to create new, but different, middle-tier jobs. In the meantime there are 'transaction costs' (pain and disruption) that have to be weathered. Others are less sanguine. They see a permanent shift in the topography of work, a global economy where investment and jobs go wherever costs are lowest.

Offshoring work is now common—from data entry, legal transcription, and call-centre services, to market research, insurance processing, and software design. Outsourcing and insourcing across borders disperses and fragments the production of goods, services, and associated jobs. Rarely now does everything get made or done in one place: we should be suspicious of product labels that proclaim 'Made in the UK' or 'Made in the USA'. Top outsourcers include the USA, Germany, and Japan, while India and China are major insourcers. However, some developing countries also outsource services. India, for example, now exports its technological and call-centre expertise to wealthier nations, such as the USA, Finland, and China. Tata, one of India's largest companies, runs call centres in the UK.

The changing profile of work has, as always, been impelled by technological innovation. Computers, robots, and software developments have diminished or supplanted many blue collar jobs—assemblers, fitters, machine operators, and welders—as well as clerical, sales, and administrative positions. In the USA, some 300,000 office and administrative support jobs disappeared in the five years before 2009, many automated away, while internet commerce has contracted high-street jobs such as banking, bookselling, travel agency, and insurance. In their wake we find a mix of people who are temporarily or permanently unemployed.

Rarely do such shifts occur noiselessly. When livelihoods are threatened, organized opposition is not uncommon. Back in 1811, Ned Ludd marked the way with his Army of Redressers ('Luddites'). They destroyed new looms in Nottingham factories, machines that replaced skilled workers with low-paid, unskilled workers. Today, Ned Ludd's spirit lives on in militant unionism and worker frustration. Occasionally, acts of sabotage are a last-ditch expression of anger or despair. For example, in 2011, in the face of worsening conditions of employment and job loss, workers in Poland's Fiat plant in Tychy damaged 300 cars by putting screws in their engines, scratching paintwork, and cutting cables.

Without work

The loss of a job can be a major life change, especially in times of economic austerity. Mergers, acquisitions, downsizing, plant closures, and societal restructuring nearly always result in redundancy programmes—now common to workforces in both Western and Eastern nations. Indeed, China's remarkable economic expansion in the late twentieth century involved abandoning a historical policy of lifetime employment. The major employers— state-owned enterprises—were dismantled and millions of workers lost their jobs. The sudden absence of a collective ethos and job security meant that many were cast adrift in the new economy.

The human consequences of job loss are rarely factored into the economic logic of organizational downsizing or retrenchment. Since the 1930s social scientists have drawn attention to the social, emotional, as well as material effects of job loss. Grief-like symptoms are not uncommon: shock, confusion, anger, denial, and depression. The impact of seeking work in a tight or retracting job market can test the coping and confidence of the most resilient of job seekers. Here three of them tell their stories, in recent recession-blighted USA:

I know I am getting close to my breaking point as I have nowhere to go and no money to go anywhere else. I am almost 60, very physically and mentally fit, have a master's degree in a field that I no longer wish to pursue, have spent the past 5 years in retail. I really want to become a paralegal and willing to go to work in any office because it has been 20 + years since I actually worked in a law office. I have worked continually since then but in various venues. I just want a job that pays enough so I as a single adult can reasonably live! And, now I have several months of past due payments for house, lot rent, $600 to get the gas turned back on, and tags expired on the car. H-E-E-L-L-P-P-P-P-P!!!!!!!!!

I am 52 years old. In April 2008 my company closed. It took me 14 years to make $40 an hour as a flight attendant. Where can I go at my age and stay afloat? I am a single woman trying to update my skills in order to compete. It is very difficult to find employment. It feels like the Big Depression. My unemployment is almost gone and I lack health insurance. God bless America.

I am a single mom of three great kids. I lost my job and can't
find another one. I have a college degree and solid work history.
I can't even get hired at Walmart or McDonald's. I now live off the
government, which I hate. I want to work and I see some of these
other people that have or have gotten the jobs I applied for and
I don't get it. My car is falling apart. I can't afford to take care of my
dogs. I'm scared living like this. It is very trying! I have a degree in
aviation and I haven't worked a day in the field since I got my licence.

Ageism emerges as one the many barriers to employment; the
over-50s are particularly vulnerable. But, in difficult times, so are
the young, as the growth of NEETs reveals.

NEETs

NEET is an acronym that appeared in the UK in the late 1990s.
It refers to young people who are 'not in education, employment or
training' for at least six months. NEETs now feature, in one form or
another, in the unemployment statistics of various countries. By
the end of 2011, the number of NEETs in the UK had risen to over
a million. In Japan in that year there were more than 640,000
NEETs, the result of major structural changes in the mid-2000s.
Then, jobs were drastically cut for young people to protect the
jobs of older workers, the final vestiges of the lifetime-employment
principle. The NEET phenomenon is relatively new to advanced
economies, but elsewhere, especially the global south, it has
long been endemic. Few 15–19-year-olds in the poorest countries
have paid employment (they may do unpaid agricultural or
domestic work), and few have moved beyond primary education.

In the UK, NEETs are a diverse group that crosses the social
spectrum: there are NEETs with university degrees and NEETs with
little more than basic school qualifications. Nevertheless, the
likelihood of becoming a NEET increases significantly with social
disadvantage. Troubled schooling, learning difficulties, and a history
of truancy edge young people closer to NEET life. NEETs have often

disengaged from mainstream society as post-16 options appear progressively unattractive or unattainable. Many have parents who are out of work, are poorly educated, and lack interest in their children's attainments. Some NEETs are also parents themselves.

NEETs have been referred to variously as the socially excluded, the marginalized, even the lost generation. They have little power or voice, which is typically how they come to see themselves—as a recent Scottish study documents:

> Unemployed 20-year-old: '…it has been over a year since I left college and I have had exactly 2 interviews. I have been told far too many times that I was unsuccessful due to my lack of experience, though I do not know how I am supposed to get experience when I hardly ever get as far as an interview…'

> Unemployed 23-year-old: '…it's so hard to get a job and when you do find a good job you need experience and there are usually about another 100 people after it.'

> Unemployed 20-year-old: 'I feel I should be doing more with my life at my age but financially, I just cannot afford to do anything because I have to claim benefits. I hate being on benefits. I feel like I have no pride in myself anymore.'

Time is an unforgiving master for NEETs: the longer they are without work, the less attractive they are to employers. Many become disaffected, depressed, and suffer low self-esteem, eventually giving up what seems a hopeless quest to find work. In an interview study of over 750 NEETs, the vast majority felt their life was wasted. Some were seriously depressed and one in four had contemplated suicide.

Turbulent transitions

NEETs are of particular concern to market economists and politicians, because their inactivity is seen to drain society of its available resources. NEET life can lock cohorts of young people into a long period (sometimes a lifetime) of dependency on the state, on their families, or both.

The situation is complicated—or eased—by the way transitions from school to work are organized. In some nations the mechanisms are well planned and firmly institutionalized. Germany and some Nordic countries, for example, have long prioritized vocational education and workplace apprenticeships for the skilled trades, crafts, and professions—all essential prerequisites to securing a job. But elsewhere, the pathways of support for school leavers have been patchy and often reactive. In the UK, NEETs are expected to take personal responsibility for their future and job search, and engage with any temporary assistance or short 'work experience' scheme that may be available. It has been a controversial approach given the difficulty in guaranteeing suitable work experience, and the raising of expectations for continuing employment, expectations that often cannot be met.

More generally, the elusiveness of jobs has meant that many young people no longer expect their occupational identities to be fixed by age 15 or thereabouts. More accessible and more attractive identities are available—such as through music, gang membership, fashion, or leisure. Entry into an uncertain or unappealing labour market can be deferred or stalled, and some young people choose to move in and out of the educational system, putting off any choices that bind them.

From *hikikomori* to freeter

One reaction by teenagers to the turbulence in the job market has been complete withdrawal. In Japan, it has been estimated that up to a million young men and women shut themselves away from all social contact:

One morning when he was 15, Takeshi shut the door to his bedroom, and for the next four years he did not come out. He didn't go to school. He didn't have a job. He didn't have friends. Month after month, he spent 23 hours a day in a room no bigger than a king-size mattress, where he ate dumplings, rice and other leftovers that his mother had cooked, watched TV game shows and listened to Radiohead and Nirvana. 'Anything,' he said, 'that was dark and sounded desperate.'

Turning inwards to escape the world's pressures has been termed *hikikomori* in Japan. Initially considered to be a unique product of Japanese culture, *hikikomori* is now viewed as generational, afflicting youths born after 1970 in many developed nations. It has been described as a modern-type depression, triggered by the increasing stress on individual achievement at ever younger ages. In Japan it typically affects adolescents from middle-class backgrounds with supportive parents. Many have not succeeded in the highly competitive, rote-learning, ethos of the Japanese educational system. Failure is a stigma that, for some *hikikomori*, has attracted the attention of bullies at school. Emotional and physical withdrawal is their way of coping, a reaction which, if unchecked, can seal their fate for years to come.

There are, in contrast, Japanese youths who have taken, arguably, a more positive approach to the changing times—as *freeters*. Much like 'Generation X' and gap-year students in the West, freeters have sought a more casual relationship with the labour market, often rejecting their parents' values of company loyalty and hard work. They have valued experimenting with different lifestyles, engaging in leisure pursuits, and enjoying the freedom from long-term commitments. Unlike *hikikomori*, freeters often do work, but typically in flexible and temporary jobs, such as convenience stores, telephone sales, and the food-service industry. Nearly 50 per cent of 15–24-year-olds were officially designated as freeters in 2006. A freeter explains:

I ended up being a freeter because I did not have the will to study right after finishing high school, and wanted to explore life, hang around. I eventually thought that I would go to college, but I did not have a clear schedule of when. My parents did not like it at all, but did not lecture me that much since I worked 5 or more times a week. I would hang around the streets with my friends at night, work during the day, catch up on sleep when I had the time, and just lived on.

Underemployment

The reshaped labour market has created a growing population of underemployed workers. People feel underemployed when their job fails to make the most of their skills, qualifications, or experience. They feel underemployed when they have insufficient work to do because their jobs are part-time or temporary. Underemployment happens in good and bad economic times, but is most evident in a weak job market. It can happen to new entrants to the labour market, as well as re-entrants. People laid off in their fifties and seeking work are often left with little choice other than basic positions, well beneath their abilities and experience.

Official labour statistics rarely distinguish between the employed and the underemployed. After all, the underemployed are in work, and common wisdom suggests that being underemployed should be preferable to having no job at all. This, however, obscures the personal and social impact of underemployment. Underemployed workers are generally discontented workers— bored and keen to quit. Working below one's capacities and skills can exact a psychological and physical toll: demoralization, stress, illness. For some, underemployment can be worse than unemployment. For instance, it has been shown that new graduates' hopes and aspirations about their chosen career remain reasonably intact (if unrealistic) if they have managed to survive an initial year without taking the only jobs on offer—

typically low skilled or menial. In comparison, those who have had to take any work that is available—in shops, restaurants, or routine clerical positions—describe how depressed they feel. They are confused about their identities having lost much of their ambition and optimism.

Migrant workers are often hit hard by underemployment. Throughout their long history, migrant workers have shored up global capitalism, but with ambiguous status: wanted but not wanted. Many struggle to find employment that matches their abilities and education, so they trade off their aspirations for the economic security of low-skilled work. To an employer, migrants can appear an irresistible source of cheap and willing labour.

Status degradation accompanies much migrant work. In Scotland, for instance, fully trained foreign nurses can be found working as care assistants; qualified engineers as kitchen helpers. In Canada there are immigrants who outstrip native-born Canadians in higher-degree qualifications, yet have ended up working in Starbucks or driving taxis. As one, a Columbian-trained engineer explained, there is a demand for engineers in his part of Canada; however, he cannot get an engineering job: 'it's more like fear; they don't believe we have the same training or the same capacities.'

Many migrants join a floating population of service workers, reinforcing a service economy on which we have come to depend. Their underemployment is fuelled by employers' doubts (frequently ill founded) about the quality of their qualifications, and by the threat they unwittingly pose to local workers: 'foreigners taking our jobs', 'undercutting our pay'. These sentiments strike an ironic note given that many of the jobs that migrants take are not ones that indigenous workers want to do.

Internship

Internship has become a contentious topic in recent years. An internship is a short period—several months to a year—of supervised job experience for a student or recent graduate, which may or may not lead to a job offer in the host organization. It has long been a feature of undergraduate programmes in the USA and the UK, and post-education internships have grown steadily in importance as a prerequisite for a full-time job. Internships provide work familiarity and CV enhancement, and can help young people make better-informed decisions on their career. They are a common first step into the 'glamorous' professions, such as theatre, film, journalism, and politics, where 'a great experience'—but no promise of a job—is offered to interns. In the USA, the prevalence of internships has spawned a mini-industry of advisers who, for a fee, offer to place interns with suitable companies.

On the face of it, an internship is an excellent, low-risk, way for an employer to invest in potential new recruits, and for the novice to gain first-hand experience of work that interests them. Well-organized, employer-committed, internships have often delivered in this win-win way. The mounting critique has been directed, not at internship's basic principles, but at the way that it has been abused by a growing number of employers, eager to exploit an oversupply of well-qualified applicants. There are accounts of companies replacing full-time paid trainees with unpaid interns, sometimes on a rolling-shift basis. Many interns work for only minimal expenses, thus a source of cheap labour—an attractive prospect for an employer in difficult economic times.

A track record of relevant internships has now become more a necessity than a luxury for a move into a career post, so those who have been unable to augment their CVs in this manner can find themselves stranded in low-level positions. The money factor looms large. Shortage of money underlines the intern's vulnerability and compounds their insecurities:

I've just started my third internship. At the end of it, I will have been working unpaid for a year. It feels as though I am not in control of my own life, that I am helpless. Academic achievements and work experience are almost irrelevant when you're competing against people who have years of experience, many of whom are taking a step down the ladder. I'm not picky—I've spent time in a children's charity, events management, a press office—but to no avail. It's demoralizing....After clocking off, most people can be free for the night. For the unpaid intern, it's time to head home and look for work.

Some interns manage by taking out loans and working part-time during unsocial hours. But the most sought-after internships, such as in national government and policy-making, are often closed to poorer applicants. The positions go predominantly to the well heeled from exclusive social networks: it is who you, or your parents, know that shapes the social hierarchy of internships. Remedying this state of affairs spotlights the role of regulation in defining interns as contributing employees to be remunerated as such, at no less than a legally minimum wage. It also involves a robust challenge to employers to reward ability, not social position and background, in disbursing internships.

...and retirement

There is a widely held expectation that we will spend a fair proportion of our later life in retirement. Popular portrayals are typically glossy: a time for well-deserved leisure and choice; of relaxation, of 'golf, fun, and eternal Sundays'. Conveniently omitted is the prospect of illness, incapacity, or poverty. Historically speaking, the notion of retirement is relatively recent, a corollary of modern, regulated industry. Prior to that, there was no official end to one's labours. For the vast majority, work stopped when they were too old or too infirm, much the same as it is today for subsistence communities in North and Sub-Saharan Africa, Asia, and the Middle East. Retirement does not figure.

In advanced economies, retirement schemes and pensions have cushioned the economic losses of stopping work. In the early days these were designed to cover a comparatively short period, given that death followed not long after retirement. In 1908, the inaugural year of the UK state pension, the retirement age was set at 70, while average life expectancy was 50. Today, the average life expectancy of men in the UK is 78, and women 82. They reflect a strong trend in population ageing in all developed countries.

Longevity represents a remarkable achievement in improved social and medical care, diet, and sanitation. But it severely challenges traditional assumptions about when, and how long, someone stays working, and how retirement is to be funded and experienced. Occupational and state pensions cannot support an ever-growing percentage of retired people who are living longer, against a background of a shrinking proportion of young people in the workforce to fund the pension system. The common counsel to younger people is to save substantially more for their future, but, for a swelling cohort of hard-pressed youngsters, the message falls on deaf ears. Many cannot find work, are poorly paid, or worry that the financial service industry will not deliver on its long-term promises: 'So what's the point of saving?'

For a growing number of workers retirement has become a complex matter. The very notion of retirement is thrown into question as mandatory retirement ages are abandoned, state-pension ages increased, and patterns of work re-formed. Relatively well-off older workers have been fairly insulated, some happily taking advantage of continuing employment into later age. But the outlook has been bleaker for poorer workers in physically or psychologically demanding jobs. They face the uncomfortable prospect of retiring without sufficient funds or pension or, if they are able, continuing in their existing job with its stresses and pressures. Their alternatives, such as shifting to less-demanding work, are limited. There are not many employers who welcome older workers, despite the growth of age-discrimination legislation,

'When I'm 65'

There are still people who retire 'normally' from long career-posts at the age of 60 or 65, some on substantial pensions. What is their retirement experience like? Initially, this rather depends on how they have felt about their previous job. When the job has been oppressive, empty of meaning or satisfaction, a common reaction is huge relief. Accounts abound of re-energized people, 'busier than ever', and turning latent or neglected talents into daily 'work'. There are 'third age' educational events, products, and services, as well as new lifestyles to contemplate.

The retirement industry has geared accordingly, encouraging consumption. Many of its outlets concentrate on a feel-good factor. Old Guys Rule, for example, focuses on a wide range of special T-shirts, headgear, and other apparel that conspicuously display the company's name. They pedal an upbeat, saccharin, vision of old age:

> A badge of honor.
>
> There comes a time in your life when comfort meets substance. When all your hard work seems to have paid dividends, and the world is at your command. All the things you hoped you could do someday, you're doing. The toils of youth are now your experiences…no longer the student, but the teacher.
>
> To celebrate your accomplishments we offer up 'Old Guys Rule' to be worn as a badge of honor for a life well spent, but not nearly over…

There is a keen commercial eye on well-off baby boomers. Property, travel, cars, boats, health aids, and financial investments are amongst their offerings for an *active* retirement. The 'busy ethic' permeates much of this discourse, buttressed by accounts of extraordinary feats of people in their sixties, seventies, and eighties, such as climbing mountains, trekking through jungles, and cycling huge distances. Ways of keeping active play to older people's anxieties about illness and physical deterioration, although marketers have been inventive in how they segment the retiree population. As, for example, 'healthy indulgers' (they like travel, home care services, and town houses), 'frail reclusers' (need overdraft protection, exercise equipment, and home health care), and 'ailing outgoers' (require investment products, health club membership, and special clothing).

When work substantially defines your identity, its ending can come as a shock—a loss of standing, meaning, and daily rhythm. Any initial euphoria can give way to unease and dislocation as a meaningful life-role fails to materialize. The absence of status props and automatic, daily, demands can leave some (especially professional and executive retirees) without a focal point in their lives. For many women, defaulting to a full-time domestic role can be an unwelcome prospect. Retirement, moreover, can be a stark reminder of mortality, thoughts suppressed in the daily routines of work life. An ex-senior manager reflects: 'Let's face it, when one retires, one is saying one has entered the final phase of life. This is it. There is no more after this…you are walking down the last corridor.' Retirees can begin to see themselves as outsiders, increasingly a burden to others and no longer contributing members of society. The accent on youth adds to their estrangement.

But admitting these feelings—to self or others—can be problematic, especially when retirement is 'supposed' to be so very different. Some deal with their dissonance by impression management: pretending that all is well. Others lean on nostalgia. There are retirees who readily describe themselves by their last job and prior identity, valorizing their past achievements. But managing retirement in these ways is precarious. One way out, for some, is to unretire, in part or whole; to work, for example, in voluntary or advisory roles. Those who have taken this path typically feel more confident and positive about life. And there are studies that indicate that, compared to people who stop working completely (and regardless of their health before retirement), they end up with fewer major diseases and can function better on a daily basis.

Never retire?

There are people for whom the very idea of retirement is irrelevant, even anathema. This is not because that they cannot afford to retire, but because their work is far more than 'a job'. It is a passion; an essential part of themselves. And importantly, it is not dependent on a single employer, or perhaps any employer. There are freelancers who fit this picture, people who jealously guard their independence and firmly reject the notion of retirement:

> As freelancers, we know that our work experience is only limited by the amount of time we spend pursuing our goals. While the ability to simply 'stop' at the end of a career may seem appealing to some, I'd much rather have the opportunity to continue doing something I love on a part-time (reduced hours) basis which keeps my mind in shape and allows me an opportunity to travel and remain socially active (while getting paid). Who'd want to retire in that position? Certainly not me, and that's why I never want to retire!

The 'never retire' refrain is common amongst creative workers. Many develop their skills over a lifetime and cannot imagine not doing what they do, even in the face of infirmity or periodic creative blocks. There are academics who feel this way—who formally retire from their college or university, but the core of their creative work continues in their writing and lecturing. Their intellectual curiosity bubbles away, not permanently parked because of some arbitrary retirement date. There are artists, actors, musicians, film makers, and novelists who have long ducked retirement, some driven on by sheer hubris, others because it is their best creative time. At 78, celebrated jazz musician and composer Quincy Jones remains sharply focused:

> I've still got a lot of energy and I want to do what my dreams are, which is to see people come together across the barriers...I'll slow down when I die.

And at 80, actor and director Clint Eastwood is puzzled that anyone in his profession should even contemplate retirement:

> I figure your best years should be at a point when you've got a lot of so-called knowledge. But there's a Portuguese director who's still making films, and he's over 100 years old. I plan to do the same.

Chapter 9
Where does this leave work? A brief postscript

In this book I have tried to reveal some of the curiosities and complexities of work—psychologically and socially. I write at a time when the fragility of work is exposed in major economic upheavals. The ripples of the 2007 sub-prime financial crisis in the USA continue to be felt across much of the globe, sharpened in Europe by its own financial difficulties. Some Eurozone countries have been unable to meet their spiralling governmental debts and have responded by radically cutting public services and jobs. Meanwhile, industries retrench in an attempt to deal with a collapse in market confidence. Shortages of work have become solid cultural realities, at times threatening societal cohesion. For many, the future does not look bright.

The decline in traditional, large-scale, manufacturing in the West continues apace, closing factories that have been at the heart of local communities for many decades. They leave in their wake broken neighbourhoods and displaced workers. But, such are the twists and turns of the global economy, that the very same factories can reappear, often under new ownership, in different parts of globe where labour costs are lower and employment regulations more relaxed.

These major disruptions reveal, in stark clarity, a theme that is central to this book: how work, in one sense or another, defines who we are and where we belong. It is an especially urgent task for educators, employers, and politicians alike to make these realizable ends—particularly for a new generation of school and university leavers, but also for those who, through no fault of their own, are separated prematurely (and often unceremoniously) from their means of livelihood.

On a less gloomy note, work and its divisions are constantly being reinvented. One era's industrial decline is overshadowed by the next one's new products and services. The future of work—if that is not too grand a term—is seeded in the structural and demographic changes discussed in this book. While globalization and outsourcing robs some people of work, it creates jobs and wealth for others, often where they are much needed, such as in developing countries. But we cannot be complacent about how this operates: the spectre of the sweatshop is an arresting one, exposing the myth of ethical business in some major corporations, as well as the weaknesses of regulation.

Much is made of the service sector as a new dawn in employment in the West—a truth that many of us observe in our high streets and on internet web pages. Jobs in retail, transport, finance, and food have sprung up to fill some of the gaps left after the demise of the manufacturing sector. They have provided opportunities for business professionals of various sorts, as well as numerous lower-skilled jobs. Now the redundant lathe or steel worker, car assembler, or supervisor can be redeployed in an out-of-town supermarket or call centre. But this, of course, is far from like-for-like, and puts human flesh on the realities of macroeconomic 'adjustments'. Service work for many ex-manufacturing employees brings a loss of pride and community, as well as a drop in income. Men, long used to the camaraderie and 'real work' in the old industries, can find a cleanly dressed life amidst the supermarket shelves alienating, even shameful. For some, the pill is too bitter to swallow—they remain unemployed.

The growing elite of the twenty-first century are knowledge workers—people with enhanced or cutting-edge knowledge and expertise. Knowledge work is fuelled by advanced research and education, so universities and research institutes play a key role in its emerging patterns. Knowledge workers are behind innovations in medicine, new drugs, synthetic biology, the next generation of iPods, iPads, and smartphones, new car design, nano technology, green technologies, and cloud computing. Entrepreneurial leaders in these fields thrive because of their creative minds and business verve, forming, as well as destroying, companies: it can be an aggressive business.

Expectations about work have changed, and will doubtless continue to do so. Workers are learning to be far more flexible and inventive in shaping their careers, and employers to be more malleable in their employment policies. Together, these actions are reshaping how much one works, where one works, and how work is divided in the family. Gender issues are becoming ever more salient as traditional male empires begin slowly to crumble. And older workers' equivocal position in the workforce ('they block jobs for the young', 'they should be out there spending their savings and pensions') is likely to ease as the economy eases. In principle, they bring not only their experience to a mixed generational workforce, but define a new zeitgeist on what a normal working lifetime will be as the population ages.

Crystal-ball gazing about work is no exact science, but one recent, and final, image heralds a possible sea change in how business will be conducted—for the better. Thousands of young people encamped in Liberty Square in Manhattan's Financial District in September 2011, and stayed there—to be followed by similar, Occupy Movement, gatherings in other American cities and across the globe. They professed to be 'fighting back against the corrosive power of major banks and multinational corporations over the democratic process, and the role of Wall Street in creating an economic collapse that has caused the greatest recession in generations'. They aimed 'to expose how the richest 1 per cent of people are writing the rules of an unfair global economy that is foreclosing on our future'.

The uprising articulated a strong public mood of distrust in the banking system, and disquiet about how wealth is distributed after the failure of the trickle-down effect. Trickle-down is a favoured, conservative, economic philosophy that asserts that giving tax breaks and economic benefits to the wealthy will ultimately benefit poorer, needy, members of society. Wealth will 'trickle down' in the form of stimulated economic growth and new jobs. In reality, much of the trickle-down appears to have been staunched more or less at source, resulting in huge accumulations of wealth amongst the relatively few.

This generational movement may achieve a much-needed shot in the arm for the ethics of business. When greed is good and numbers on a screen enclose the world of the corporate worker, decision-makers are insulated from their impact on others, and from any obligations to the wider community. It is a breeding ground for malpractice, as a litany of corporate scandals shows. If the Movement's legacy is to keep these issues to the forefront of public and private policy, then that is certainly something worth celebrating.

References

Chapter 1: Why work?

J. Goldthorpe, D. Lockwood, F. Bechhofer, and J. Pratt, *The Affluent Worker in the Class Structure* (Cambridge: Cambridge University Press, 1969).

G. Grandin, *Fordlandia: The Rise and Fall of Henry Ford's Forgotten Jungle City* (Singapore: Icon Books, 2010), 222.

N. A. Hira, 'You Raised Them, Now Manage Them', *Fortune*, 155 (9) (2007): 38.

C. Marston, *Mixing Four Generations in the Workforce* (Topsfield, Mass.: Enterprise Media, 2010).

A. Maslow, 'A Theory of Human Motivation', *Psychological Review*, 50 (1943): 370–96.

D. McGregor, *The Human Side of Enterprise* (London: McGraw-Hill, 1960).

T. Watson, *Organising and Managing Work* (Upper Saddle River, NJ: Pearson Education, 2002), 278.

M. Weber, *The Protestant Ethic and the Spirit of Capitalism* (New York: Scribner, 1958).

The news report of the lucky bus driver can be found in the *Chorley Guardian*, 'Chorley Lottery Winner Won't Give up Day Job', 17 March 2010, <http://www.chorley-guardian.co.uk>.

Chapter 2: A spectrum of jobs

P. F. Drucker. *The Age of Discontinuity* (London: Harper and Row, 1969), 264.

I. Brinkley, *Defining the Knowledge Economy: Knowledge Economy Programme Report* (London: The Work Foundation, 2006).

The social class ascriptions are located in the *Annual British Social Attitudes Survey* (National Centre for Social Research, 2007).

Figure 3. Average salaries: reported in the *Annual Survey of Hours and Earnings*, 'Occupation (4), Table 14.7a. Annual Pay, Gross 2010', Office of National Statistics, UK Statistics Authority. I have added the salary for management consultants from 'Salary Benchmarking Report 2011/2012', *Top-Consultant.com*, and for football managers from *Trophy4toon*, <http://www.trophy4toon. co.uk/salaries.html>.

Chapter 3: Working a career

J. Allen and N. Henry, 'Ulrich Beck's Risk Society at Work: Labour and Employment in the Contract Service Industries', *Transactions of the Institute of British Geographers*, 22 (2) (1997): 191.

M. Arthur, 'The Boundaryless Career: A New Perspective for Organizational Inquiry', *Journal of Organizational Behaviour*, 15 (1994): 295–306.

C. Handy, *The Age of Unreason* (Cambridge, Mass.: Harvard Business Review Press, 1989), 147.

P. Toynbee, *Hard Work* (London: Bloomsbury, 2003), 96–7.

W. H. Whyte, *The Organization Man* (New York: Simon and Schuster, 1956), 130.

The voices opening this chapter are from W. S. Brown, 'The New Employment Contract and the "at Risk" Worker', *Journal of Business Ethics*, 58 (1) (2005): 199, 200.

Figure 4 is adapted from S. E. Sullivan, 'The Changing Nature of Careers: A Review and Research Agenda', *Journal of Management*, 25 (3) (1999): 457–84.

The notion of a 'precariat' is discussed by G. Standing in his book *The Precariat: The New Dangerous Class* (London: Bloomsbury Academic, 2011).

Chapter 4: Men's work, women's work

K. Deaux, and T. Emswiller, 'Explanations of Successful Performance on Sex-Linked Tasks: What is Skill for the Male is Luck for the Female', *Journal of Personality and Social Psychology*, 29 (1) (1974): 80–5.

C. Hakim, *Key Issues in Women's Work* (Blanco, Tex.: The Glass House Press, 2004).

A. C. Pigou, *The Economics of Welfare* (Piscataway, NJ: Transaction Publishers, 1952), 33.

The Foreign Office tale is reported in H. Martindale, *Women Servants of the State* (London: Allen and Unwin, 1938), 34.

Figure 7 is adapted from *US Bureau of Labor Statistics, 2011*, <www.bls.gov/cps/cpsaat11.pdf>.

Figure 8 is from *Gender Brief*, OECD, March 2010, 13. <http://www.oecd.org/dataoecd/23/31/44720649.pdf>.

The London working-wife's comment is published in *MailOnline*, 28 August 2010. It is her response to a *Mail* article, 'Myth of the "New Man" is Exposed: Men are Doing No More Housework than 30 Years Ago'.

The quote from the woman about her first day on a construction site is in S. Eisenberg, *We'll Call You if We Need You: Experiences of Women Working Construction* (Ithaca, NY: Cornell University Press, 1999), 132.

The women engineers' views about how they deal with a male culture are in A. Powell, B. Bagilhole, and A. Dainty, 'How Women Engineers Do and Undo Gender: Consequences for Gender Equality', *Gender, Work & Organization*, 16 (4) (2009): 411–28.

The quote from a 'token' woman director is accessible at <http://www.womenonboards.org.au/boardroom/cs/cook-jackie.htm>.

'Women at the top'. Evidence on the influence of women on boards of directors can be found in several studies: *Women on Boards* (Paris: McKinsey, 2011); L. Joy, N. Carter, H. Wagener, and S. Narayanan, *Performance and Women's Representation on Boards* (New York: Catalyst, 2007); and N. Wilson, *Women in the Boardroom Help Companies Succeed*, Leeds University Business School, reported in *The Times*, 19 March 2009.

The Swedish study of a large number of company boards is reported in 'Beyond the Glass Ceiling: Does Gender Matter?' by R. Adams and P. Funk, Working Papers (Universitat Pompeu Fabra, Departamento de Economía y Empresa).

McJobs and 'McDonaldization' are attributable to G. Ritzer, *The McDonaldization of Society* (Thousand Oaks, Calif.: Pine Forge Press, 1993).

The Western Electric studies are reported in F. J. Roethlisberger, W. J. Dickson, and H. A. Wright, *Management and the Worker* (Cambridge, Mass.: Harvard University Press, 1939).

The humour case study of a British software firm is '"Don't get me wrong, it's fun here, but…": Ambivalence and Paradox in a "Fun" Work Environment', by S. Warren and S. Fineman, in R. Westwood, and C. Rhodes (eds.), *Humour, Work and Organization* (London: Routledge, 2007), 92–112.

The original account of Type A personality was by M. Friedman and R. Rosenman, in their edited book *Type A Behavior and your Heart* (New York: Alfred A. Knopf, 1974).

Chapter 6: Emotion at work

D. Goleman, *Emotional Intelligence* (London: Bloomsbury, 1995).

A. Hochschild, *The Managed Heart* (Berkeley and Los Angeles: University of California Press, 1983), 127.

M. Weber, *Economy and Society*, Vol. 2 (Somerville, NJ: Bedminster Press, 1968), 75.

The manager talking about his decision-making is reported in D. J. Isenberg, 'How Senior Managers Think', *Harvard Business Review*, 62 (2) (1984): 87.

The scene from McDonald's extracted from BBC Channel 2 television film on 'empowerment' for the Open University, 1998.

The Brooklyn Burger King manager is reported in J. T. Talwar, *Fast Food, Fast Track* (Boulder, Colo.: Westview Press, 2002), 114.

The study on the proportion of employees bullied is '20% of UK workers have been bullied over the last 2 years—with highest levels reported in the public sector', reported by the Chartered Institute of Personnel and Development, 24 October 2006. <http://www.cipd.co.uk/pressoffice/_articles/bullying241006.htm>.

The *Guardian* observation on the life of a hotel maid (plus comments on the Straus-Kahn case) is by D. Rusche, 'New York Maids Demand to be Heard as they Dish the Dirt on Hotel Life', *The Guardian*, 10 June 2011.

Chapter 7: Virtual work

The expansive personal account of story cyberbullying is reported in *RespectU.com*, <http://www.respectu.com/work.php>.

The Australian study of cyberbullying amongst manufacturing employees is by C. Privitera and M. A. Campbell, 'Cyberbullying: The New Face of Workplace Bullying?' *CyberPsychology and Behavior*, 22 (4) (2009): 395–400.

The cyberbullying of teachers in the UK is evidenced in a teachers' union survey (NASUWT), reported in *The Guardian*, 7 April 2012, 17.

Chapter 8: Changes and transitions

The Scottish study of NEETs is 'Being Young Being Heard', published by Citizens Advice Scotland (February 2011), <http://www.cas.org.uk>.

The interview study of NEETs is 'UK Youth Feels Consigned to Life on the Scrapheap', published by *Future You* (2011), <http://www.thefutureyou.org.uk>.

The account of Takeshi, the young Japanese *hikikomori*, is by M. Jones, 'Shutting Themselves in', *New York Times* (15 January 2006).

Further reading

Chapter 1: Why work?

On work meanings and motivation:

S. Fineman, Y. Gabriel, and D. Sims, *Organizing and Organizations*, 4th edn. (New York: Sage, 2010).

G. P. Latham, *Work Motivation: History, Theory, Research, and Practice* (New York: Sage, 2012).

On the Protestant Work Ethic:

A. Furnham, *The Protestant Work Ethic: The Psychology of Work-Related Beliefs and Behaviours* (London: Routledge, 1992).

On age and generations:

S. Fineman, *Organizing Age* (Oxford: Oxford University Press, 2011).

F. Giancola, 'The Generation Gap: More Myth than Reality', *Human Resource Planning*, 29 (4) (2006): 32.

Chapter 2: A spectrum of jobs

On the black economy and migrant labour:

T. Shelley, *Exploited: Migrant Labour in the New Global Economy* (London: Zed Books, 1988).

A. Venkatesh, *Off the Books: The Underground Economy of the Urban Poor* (Cambridge, Mass.: Harvard University Press, 2008).

On knowledge work:

A. P. Botha, *Knowledge: Living and Working with It* (Claremont: Juta & Company, 2008).

On status and social class:

R. Hodson and T. A. Sullivan, *The Social Organization of Work* (Independence, Ky.: Wadsworth, 2012).

A. Lareau and D. Conley, *Social Class: How Does it Work?* (New York: Russell Sage Foundation, 2008).

On industrial democracy and trade unions:

E. Rose, *Employment Relations* (New York: Prentice Hall, 2008).

A. Wilkinson, P. J. Gollan, and M. Marchington, *The Oxford Handbook of Participation in Organizations* (Oxford: Oxford University Press, 2010).

On Walmart:

T. J. Adams, 'Walmart and the Making of "Postindustrial Society"', *Labor*, 8 (1) (2011): 117–25.

Chapter 3: Working a career

On new types of career:

M. Arthur, K. Inkson, and J. K. Pringle, *The New Careers: Individual Action and Economic Change* (New York: Sage, 2003).

H. Gunz, and M. Peiperl, *Handbook of Career Studies* (New York: Sage, 2007).

On employability:

M. Clarke, 'Plodders, Pragmatists, Visionaries and Opportunists: Career Patterns and Employability', *Career Development International*, 14 (1) (2009): 8–28.

On contingent workers:

B. Ehrenreich, *Nickel and Dimed: On (not) Getting By in America* (New York: Holt, 2008).

D. G. Gallagher, 'I pledge thee my troth . . . contingently: Commitment and the Contingent Work Relationship', *Human Resource Management Review*, 11 (3) (2001): 181–208.

On flexible employment:

D. M. Rousseau, *I-Deals, Idiosyncratic Deals Employees Bargain for Themselves* (Armonk, NY: M. E. Sharpe, 2005).

E. Skorstad and H. Ramsdal (eds.), *Flexible Organizations and the New Working Life: A European Perspective* (Aldershot: Ashgate, 2009).

Chapter 4: Men's work, women's work

On gender and work in Saudi Arabia:

R. Lacey, *Inside the Kingdom* (London: Arrow Books, 2010).

On women in businesses:

M. E. Reeves, *Women in Business: Theory, Case Studies, and Legal Challenges* (London: Routledge, 2010).

K. Salmansohn, *How to Succeed in Business without a Penis: Secrets and Strategies for the Working Woman* (Lincoln, Nebr.: Authors Choice Press, 2006).

On sexual divisions in the workplace:

I. C. Williams and K. Dellinger (eds.), *Gender and Sexuality in the Workplace* (Castle Hill: Emerald, 2010).

I. Padvic and B. Reskin, *Women and Men at Work* (Thousand Oaks, Calif.: Pine Forge, 2002).

On household work:

J. Treas and S. Drobnič (eds.), *Dividing the Domestic: Men, Women, and Household Work in Cross-National Perspective* (Stanford, Calif.: Stanford University Press, 2010).

Chapter 5: Struggling, surviving, thriving

On the work and life of Frederick Taylor:

S. Kakar, *Frederick Taylor: A Study in Personality and Innovation* (Cambridge, Mass.: MIT Press, 1974).

On McDonaldization:

G. Ritzer, *McDonaldization: The Reader* (New York: Sage, 2010).

On humour at work:

J. Holmes and M. Marra, 'Having a Laugh at Work: How Humour Contributes to Workplace Culture', *Journal of Pragmatics*, 34 (12) (2002): 1683–710.

On empowerment and enrichment at work:

J. Martin, *Key Concepts in Human Resource Management* (New York: Sage, 2010).

E. H. Schein, 'Empowerment, Coercive Persuasion and Organizational Learning: Do They Connect?' *Learning Organization*, 6 (4) (1999): 163–72.

On presenteeism and long hours:

P. Hemp, 'Presenteeism: At Work—But out of it', *Harvard Business Review* (October 2004): 1–9.

S. A. Hewlett and C. B. Luce, 'Extreme Jobs–The Dangerous Allure of the 70-Hour Workweek', *Harvard Business Review*, 84 (12) (2006): 49–59.

On downshifting:

C. Honore, *In Praise of Slow* (Paris: Hachette, 2010).

M. McCain, *Downshifting Made Easy: How to Plan for your Planet-Friendly Future* (Oxford: John Hunt, 2011).

J. Schor, *The Overspent American: Upscaling, Downshifting, and the New Consumer* (New York: Basic Books, 1998).

On 'the positive movement':

P. Bruckner, *Perpetual Euphoria: On the Duty to Be Happy* (Princeton: Princeton University Press, 2000).

K. S. Cameron, J. E. Dutton, and R. E. Quinn (eds.), *Positive Organizational Scholarship: Foundations of a New Discipline* (San Francisco: Berrett-Koehler, 2003).

S. Fineman, 'On Being Positive: Concerns and Counterpoints', *Academy of Management Review*, 31 (2) (2006): 270–91.

Chapter 6: Emotion at work

On emotion's major concepts:

S. Fineman, *Understanding Emotion at Work* (New York: Sage, 2003).

S. Fineman (ed.), *Emotion in Organizations* (New York: Sage, 2000).

S. Fineman (ed.), *The Emotional Organization: Passions and Power* (Oxford: Blackwell, 2008).

On aesthetic labour:

A. Bryman, *The Disneyization of Society* (New York: Sage, 2004).

On emotional intelligence and its controversies:

M. Zeidner, G. Matthews, and D. Roberts, *What We Know about Emotional Intelligence* (Cambridge, Mass.: MIT, 2009).

On bullying and harassment at work:

A. Oade, *Managing Workplace Bullying: How to Identify, Respond to and Manage Bullying* (Basingstoke: Palgrave Macmillan, 2009).

E. Wall, *Sexual Harassment: Confrontations and Decisions* (Amherst, NY: Prometheus Books, 2000).

Chapter 7: Virtual work

On telework:

Y. Baruch and N. Nicholson, 'Home, Sweet Work: Requirements for Effective Home Working', *Journal of General Management*, 23 (1997): 5–30.

M. Amigoni and S. Gurvis, *Managing the Telecommuting Employee* (Erina: Adams Business, 2009).

A. Verbeke, R. Schulz, N. Greidanus, and L. Hambley, *Growing the Virtual Workplace: The Integrative Value Proposition for Telework* (Cheltenham: Edward Elgar, 2008).

On virtual teams:

Harvard Business School Press, *Leading Virtual Teams: Expert Solutions to Everyday Challenges* (Cambridge, Mass.: Harvard Business School Press, 2010).

D. L. Duarte and N. T. Snyder, *Mastering Virtual Teams: Strategies, Tools, and Techniques That Succeed* (San Francisco: Jossey-Bass, 2006).

On virtual communication:

N. Sheehy and T. Gallager, 'Can Virtual Organizations be Made Real?' *The Psychologist* (April 1996): 159–62.

J. Gackenbach (ed.), *Psychology and the Internet* (Salt Lake City: Academic Press, 1998).

On cyber incivility and bullying:

V. Bowie, B. Fisher, and C. L. Cooper, *Workplace Violence: Issues, Trends, Strategies* (London: Willan, 2005).

On personal internet usage at work:

M. Anandarajan and C. Simmers, *Personal Web Usage in the Workplace: A Guide to Effective Human Resources Management* (Hershey, Pa.: Information Science Publishing, 2004).

R. K. Garrett and J. N. Danziger, 'On Cyberslacking: Workplace Status and Personal Internet Use at Work', *CyberPsychology & Behavior*, 11 (3) (2008): 287–92.

Chapter 8: Changes and transitions

On structural shifts in the labour market:

S. Ackroyd, R. Batt, P. Thompson, and P. S. Tolbert, *The Oxford Handbook of Work and Organization* (Oxford: Oxford University Press, 2006).

M. Goos and A. Manning, 'Lousy and Lovely Jobs: The Rising Polarization of Work in Britain', *Review of Economics and Statistics*, 89 (1) (2007): 118–33.

F. Gandolfi, *Corporate Downsizing Demystified: A Scholarly Analysis of a Business Phenomenon* (New York: ICFAI Books, 2006).

R. S. Rajan and S. Srivastava, 'Global Outsourcing of Services: Issues and Implications', *Harvard Asia Pacific Review*, 9 (1) (2007): 39–40.

On unemployment and job loss:

S. Fineman (ed.), *Unemployment: Personal and Social Consequences* (London: Tavistock, 1987).

A. Furlong, *Handbook of Youth and Young Adulthood* (London: Routledge, 2009).

Y. Gabriel, D. E. Gray, and H. Goregaokar, 'Temporary Derailment or the End of the Line? Managers Coping with Unemployment at 50', *Organization Studies*, 31 (12) (2010): 1687–712.

House of Commons, *Young People Not in Education, Employment or Training*, Vol. 1 (Great Britain Parliament, 2010).

On *hikikomori* and freeters:

T. A. Kato, N. Shinfuku, N. Sartorius, and S. Kanba, 'Are Japan's Hikikomori and Depression in Young People Spreading Abroad?' *The Lancet*, 378 (9796) (2011): 1070.

R. Kosugi, 'Youth Employment in Japan's Economic Recovery: "Freeters" and "NEETs"', *Asia-Pacific Journal: Japan Focus* (11 May 2006).

M. Zielenziger, *Shutting out the Sun: How Japan Created its Own Lost Generation* (New York: Random House, 2006).

On underemployment:

D. C. Maynard and D. C. Feldman, *Underemployment: Psychological, Economic, and Social Challenges* (New York: Springer, 2011).

On internship:

J. Harker, 'What Should Work Experience Look Like?' *The Guardian* (24 February 2012).

Work

B. Staunton, 'Internships Exposed as Unemployment Rises' (24 October 2011), <http://thecourieronline.co.uk>.

B. Milligan, '"Interns Exploited by Employers", says TUC' (BBC News, 13 March 2010), <http://news.bbc.co.uk>.

On retirement:

S. Fineman, 'When I'm Sixty Five: The Shaping and Shapers of Retirement Identity and Experience', in P. Hancock and M. Tyler (eds.), *The Management of Everyday Life* (Basingstoke: Palgrave Macmillan, 2009).

S. Fineman, 'Retirement', in S. Fineman, *Organizing Age* (Oxford: Oxford University Press, 2011).

R. S. Weiss, *The Experience of Retirement* (Ithaca, NY: Cornell University Press, 2005).

Index

Work

Expand your collection of
VERY SHORT INTRODUCTIONS

ORGANIZATIONS
A Very Short Introduction
Mary Jo Hatch

This *Very Short Introductions* addresses all of these questions and considers many more. Mary Jo Hatch introduces the concept of organizations by presenting definitions and ideas drawn from the a variety of subject areas including the physical sciences, economics, sociology, psychology, anthropology, literature, and the visual and performing arts. Drawing on examples from prehistory and everyday life, from the animal kingdom as well as from business, government, and other formal organizations, Hatch provides a lively and thought provoking introduction to the process of organization.

LEADERSHIP
A Very Short Introduction
Keith Grint

In this *Very Short Introduction* Keith Grint prompts the reader to rethink their understanding of what leadership is. He examines the way leadership has evolved from its earliest manifestations in ancient societies, highlighting the beginnings of leadership writings through Plato, Sun Tzu, Machiavelli and others, to consider the role of the social, economic, and political context undermining particular modes of leadership. Exploring the idea that leaders cannot exist without followers, and recognising that we all have diverse experiences and assumptions of leadership, Grint looks at the practice of management, its history, future, and influence on all aspects of society.

www.oup.com/vsi